THE PUFFIN BOOK OF
MAGIC VERSE

Chosen and Introduced
by
Charles Causley

Illustrated by
Barbara Świderska

Kestrel Books

KESTREL BOOKS
Penguin Books Ltd
Harmondsworth, Middlesex, England

This Collection Copyright © 1974 by Charles Causley
Illustrations Copyright © 1974 by Penguin Books Ltd

First published 1974

Reissued 1981

ISBN 0 7226 5220 8

Printed in Hong Kong by
Wing Tai Cheung Printing Co. Ltd.

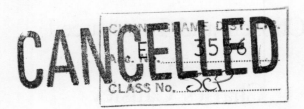

THE PUFFIN BOOK OF
MAGIC VERSE

TO

GLADYS AND F. L. HARRIS

OF REDRUTH

CONTENTS

CONTENTS

CONTENTS

CONTENTS

CHANGELINGS

GHOSTS AND HAUNTINGS

CONTENTS

ENCHANTMENTS

DWARFS, GIANTS, OGRES AND DEMONS

11

CONTENTS

CONTENTS

SALT WATER SPIRITS, FRESH WATER SPIRITS

CREATURES OF EARTH AND AIR

CONTENTS

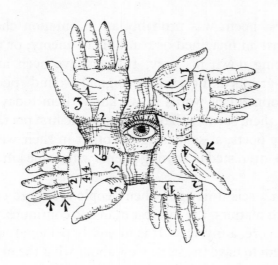

INTRODUCTION

ALL poetry is magic. It is a spell against insensitivity, failure of imagination, ignorance, and barbarism. The way that a good poem 'works' on a reader is as mysterious, as hard to explain, as the possible working of a charm or spell. A poem is much more than a mere arrangement of words on paper, or on the tongue. Its hints, suggestions, the echoes it sets off in the mind, and its omissions (what a poet decides to leave out is often just as important as what he puts in) all join up with the reader's thoughts and feelings and make a kind of magical union.

When he writes his poem, the poet is careful to make a space, a carefully unspecified area (you can't see it with the naked eye), which can be occupied by the mind and heart and imagination of the reader. Not, of course, that the poet is conscious of his audience when he is writing. At that time, he is both writer and reader, and the poem is for himself alone. Yet in just such a way, one imagines, the witches, wise ones, or 'pellers' as we sometimes call them in Cornwall, composed their spells in ways they hoped would be most successful.

The first poem was probably an incantation chanted in a cave against an imagined or real human enemy, or to help the hunter bring down his prey. It may have been made up of rhythmic grunts and cries (the original 'sound' poem) before the development of words as we know them today. The first magician, then, seems to have been also the first poet. Certainly, very many poets, at some stage or other in their writing lives, have been interested in writing poems with some kind of 'magical' theme.

Even in a scientific age, when people are more enlightened about such matters, the interest in magic continues. For magic has, at its core, a mystery. It is intensely personal; and no two people seem to have the same view about what the mystery may 'mean'.

So it is that we find a poet who was as much of his own age as W. H. Auden writing about ogres.

> Little fellow, you're amusing,
> Stop before you end by losing
>   Your shirt:
> Run along to Mother, Gus,
> Those who interfere with us
>   Get hurt.   (*page 162*)

Auden's ogres may not have been the giants of fairy-stories, but twentieth-century monsters of intolerance, greed, and suspicion. It is important to notice, all the same, that though this is a poem of menace, it is not a menacing poem. It is a poem of hope. It is, among other things, a sharp warning as to what may happen if we relax our watchfulness on the preservation of liberty.

Beneath the thin modern skin of life, beliefs in magic lie lightly sleeping, and are still very much alive. These folk-memories of our long crawl out of the prehistoric cave into the sun of reason will awaken easily. Who, for instance, has never instinctively touched wood for luck? Or not thrown a little spilled salt over his left shoulder to defeat the devil? Or tried to avoid bad luck by not walking under a ladder?

Whether or not we believe in the effectiveness of ancient charms or spells, we can hardly fail to be moved by the sheer poetry of their language. As with the traditional ballads, we shall probably now never know who wrote them. Time has worn away all their unnecessary decoration and all the dead phrasing (if they ever had any), and we are left with the clear, hard bones of poetry, as in 'Charm for a Burn or Scald'.

> There were three angels came from the East and West;
> One brought fire, and another brought frost,
> And the third, it was the Holy Ghost.
> Out fire, in frost . . .   (*page 33*)

It must be pointed out very strongly that this book contains *poems*: not remedies or cures. On no account should any of them be tried in place of a visit to a doctor or hospital, or as first-aid treatment in case of an accident. In any case, as those who call themselves charmers or witches would tell you, a charm loses its power when it is written down or published for all to see. Spells are said by them only to stay effective when words are kept secret by the 'peller', who is often the seventh child of a seventh child, or a footling (one who is born feet instead of head first) and so believed to be possessed of magic powers. The charmers also say that spells must be passed secretly by word of mouth from one person to another, from a male to a female, or from a female to a male.

I have grouped the poems that follow under ten general headings. But I think it will soon be seen that one subject, or theme, very often seems to melt into another. This, very properly, is part of the very nature of poetry. A poem is not an object, fixed in space and time, with a single, immovable 'meaning'. It is a living organism which we can study, match with our own experience of life, and of which we may make something new every day. Properly examined, a good poem, however simple-seeming it may appear on the surface, never stops giving up fresh and exciting secrets.

Incantations, curses, elves, changelings (elf or fairy children substituted for stolen human ones), wizards, ghosts, mermaids, and the like are plain enough subjects in an anthology of magic verse. But I have also included poems of the mystery and magic many poets see in the day to day events of the natural world and of everyday life: those happenings that perhaps we may too often take for granted. An Anglo-Saxon poet (p. 185) has a clear vision of the strange creatures of sun and moon. A poet of today, Edward Storey, writes of the 'kingdom of mist'.

> And night comes down where day once grew,
> lights ripple through this thin white sea,
> while in the village children sleep
> never to know they slept in sky.   (*page 188*)

Another modern poet, Leslie Norris, detects the secret magic in something as commonplace as a handful of stones.

> Once in a million years
> Their stone hearts lurch.   (*page 189*)

The similarity between the poet and the magician has always been a close one. And just as the magician dreads the loss of his powers, so the poet hopes that inspiration will not forsake him. The anonymous poet of the Gilbert Islands appeals to the sun.

> Let it fill me with light as thou,
> Let it soar above the shadows,
> Let it live!
> So shall I be eloquent.   (*page 46*)

I hope that this anthology will remind the reader that mystery and magic are not necessarily faraway things of the past, but are found here, today, close to our five senses: and to these senses we must also bring our minds and imaginations. As the

Red Indian from Omaha says in 'Song of Two Ghosts':

> My friend
> This is a wide world
> We're travelling over ...   (*page 101*)

Just what the nature of the 'other' world is – and even if it exists at all – each must decide for himself. One thing seems certain: that the language of magic always has been, always must be, the language of poetry.

CHARLES CAUSLEY

Launceston, Cornwall

Charms and Spells

CHARM FOR ST VALENTINE'S EVE

On going to bed, place your shoes in the form of a letter T, *and repeat the following verse. Then reverse the shoes, and say three times more.*

> I place my shoes like a letter T,
> In hopes my true love I shall see,
> In his apparel and his array,
> As he is now and every day.

ANONYMOUS

CHARM FOR A LOVER

To be recited on seeing the first new moon after Midsummer.

> All hail, new moon, all hail to thee!
> I prithee, good moon, reveal to me
> This night who shall my true love be;
> Who is he, and what he wears,
> And what he does all months and years.

ANONYMOUS

LOVE-CHARM SONGS

I

You magic power in the skies
who love the rains
make it so that he
no matter how many women he has
will think them all ugly
make him remember me
remember me
this afternoon
when the sun goes to the west

II

New moon
new moon
here I am in your presence
make it so
that only I
may occupy his heart

TUPI INDIANS, SOUTH AMERICA

CHARM ON SEEING A PISKY

Jack o' the lantern, Joan the wad!
Who tickled the maid, and made her mad,
Light me home, the weather's bad.

ANONYMOUS

pisky : elf or pixy
Jack o' the lantern : Will o' the wisp

CHARME

If ye feare to be affrighted
When ye are (by chance) benighted:
In your Pocket for a trust,
Carrie nothing but a Crust:
For that holy piece of Bread,
Charmes the danger, and the dread.

ROBERT HERRICK

to be benighted : to lose one's way in the dark; to be led astray by mischievous sprites

CHARME

In the morning when ye rise
Wash your hands, and cleanse your eyes.
Next be sure ye have a care,
To disperse the water farre.
For as farre as that doth light,
So farre keepes the evill Spright.

ROBERT HERRICK

CHARM AGAINST A MAGPIE

To see one magpie is thought to be unlucky. To avert possible evil, say the following after spitting three times over the right shoulder.

Clean birds by sevens,
Unclean by twos;
The dove, in the Heavens,
Is the one I choose.

ANONYMOUS

CHARME

Bring the holy crust of Bread,
Lay it underneath the head;
'Tis a certain Charme to keep
Hags away, while Children sleep.

ROBERT HERRICK

hag : female evil spirit, or witch

CHARM AGAINST AN EGG-BOAT

According to an old superstition, when a boiled egg had been eaten, the spoon at once had to be put through the end of the shell that was not yet broken. This was believed to prevent witches from going to sea in unbroken shells and brewing up storms.

You must break the shell to bits, for fear
The witches should make it a boat, my dear:
For over the sea, away from home,
Far by night the witches roam.

ANONYMOUS

See also the poem by Rudyard Kipling on p. 73.

CHARM FOR A WART

While washing the hands in the moon's rays shining in a dry metal basin, recite the following.

I wash my hands in this thy dish,
Oh man in the moon, do grant my wish,
And come and take away this.

ANONYMOUS

'THE SOUL IS THE BREATH
IN YOUR BODY'

You can sell them for a penny to
you mother

or

You can tie knots for each one
in a piece of string
and plant it at the bottom of your garden
and water it
every morning
that makes them grow under the earth

or

You can have them charmed
if you know a charmer
there are lots in Cornwall you must
leave her a gift and not say thankyou
then she will sing
an incantation

or

there is the witches way.
You take a special white round stone
for every one
and put them in a pretty red bag
into the middle of the road –

Don't touch that bag it's got
warts in it

or

If you can find the green toad you
got them from you can
give them back to him if he'll have them

or

You can rub snails on them or slugs
and if that doesn't cure them

you still want them.

JENI COUZYN

CHARME FOR STABLES

Hang up Hooks, and Sheers to scare
Hence the Hag, that rides the Mare,
Till they be all over wet,
With the mire, and the sweat:
This observ'd, the Manes shall be
Of your horses, all knot-free.

ROBERT HERRICK

CHARM FOR A THORN-PRICK

Happy man that Christ was born,
He was crowned with a thorn;
He was pierced through the skin,
For to let the poison in:
But his five wounds, so they say,
Closed before he passed away;
In with healing, out with thorn;
Happy man that Christ was born.

ANONYMOUS

CHARM FOR AN ADDER BITE

Or to make an adder destroy itself

Underneath this 'hazelen mot'
There's a braggaty worm, with a speckled throat,
Now! Nine double hath he.
Now from nine double to eight double,
From eight double, to seven double,
From seven double, to six double,
From six double, to five double,
From five double, to four double,
From four double, to three double,
From three double, to two double,
From two double, to one double,
    Now! No double hath he.

ANONYMOUS

hazelen mot : the root of a hazel tree
braggaty : spotted   *double :* a ring

RATTLESNAKE CEREMONY SONG

The king snake said to the rattlesnake:
Do not touch me!
You can do nothing with me.
Lying with your belly full,
Rattlesnake of the rock pile,
Do not touch me!
There is nothing you can do,
You rattlesnake with your belly full,
Lying where the ground-squirrel holes are thick.
Do not touch me!
What can you do to me?
Rattlesnake in the tree clump,
Stretched in the shade,
You can do nothing;
Do not touch me!
Rattlesnake of the plains,
You whose white eye
The sun shines on,
Do not touch me!

YOKUTS INDIANS, NORTH AMERICA

MAGIC SONG FOR HIM
WHO WISHES TO LIVE

Day arises
From its sleep,
Day wakes up
With the dawning light.
Also you must arise,
Also you must awake
Together with the day which comes.

ESKIMO SONG, GREENLAND

CHARM FOR THE TOOTHACHE

Christ passed by his brother's door,
Saw Peter his brother lying on the floor;
What aileth thee, brother? –
Pain in thy teeth?
Thy teeth shall pain thee no more:
In the name of the Father, Son, and Holy Ghost.

Amen

ANONYMOUS

CHARM TO STANCH BLEEDING

Jesus was born in Bethlehem,
Baptized in River Jordan, when
The water was wild in the wood,
The person was just and good;
God spake, and the water stood:
And so shall now thy blood —
In the name of the Father, Son, and Holy Ghost.
                                        Amen

ANONYMOUS

CHARM FOR A BURN OR SCALD

There were three angels came from the East and West;
One brought fire, and another brought frost,
And the third, it was the Holy Ghost.
Out fire, in frost, in the name of the Father,
        Son, and Holy Ghost.

                                        Amen

ANONYMOUS

CHARM FOR WILDFIRE

Christ, he walketh over the land,
Carried the wildfire in his hand,
He rebuked the fire, and bid it stand;
Stand, wildfire stand,
Stand, wildfire stand,
Stand, wildfire stand,
In the name of the Father, Son, and Holy Ghost.
                                        Amen

ANONYMOUS

wildfire: the skin disease erysipelas

CHARM

(*Zarze zarzyce trzy siestrzyce.*)

Rosie, rosaiden: there were three maidens.
Our Lady, Mary, walked on the sea and plucked a
    garland of gold foam.
And then Saint John came down and asked: 'Where are
    you walking, my dear?'
'I'm off to cure my son.'

ANONYMOUS, 15th century;
translated from the Polish by Jerzy Peterkiewicz
and Burns Singer

The translators say: ' "rosie, rosaiden" is an attempt to reproduce both
the play on the word *zarze* (meaning the light of dawn) and the inner
rhyme, linking *zarzyce* with *siestrzyce* (i.e., sisters).'

34

CURING SONG

Your heart is good.
(The Spirit) Shining Darkness will be here.
You think only of sad unpleasant things,
You are to think of goodness.
Lie down and sleep here.
Shining darkness will join us.
You think of this goodness in your dream.
Goodness will be given to you,
I will speak for it, and it will come to pass.
It will happen here,
I will ask for your good,
It will happen as I sit by you,
It will be done as I sit here in this place.

YUMA INDIANS, NORTH AMERICA

WEST WIND TO THE BAIRN

West wind to the bairn,
When going for its name;
And rain to the corpse,
Carried to its last hame.

A bonny blue sky,
To welcome the bride,
As she goes to the kirk,
With the sun on her side.

ANONYMOUS, SCOTTISH

SONG TO BRING FAIR WEATHER

You, whose day it is, make it beautiful.
Get out your rainbow colours,
So it will be beautiful.

NOOTKA INDIANS, NORTH AMERICA

THE ROGERY BIRDS

I heard the wind blow over the hill,
 Bolderogery-rogery-O!
And it beat and bounced and banged with a will,
 Bolderogery-rogery-O!
But I didn't care how hard it blew,
Or if it went under the hill or through,
For I was safe and sound in the house,
Cosy and warm and snug as a mouse,
 Bolderogery! Bolderogery! Bolderogery-O!

The fire was bright, for the night was cold,
 Bolderogery-rogery-O!
The flame flew up, and the sparks were gold,
 Bolderogery-rogery-O!
But out in the marsh I heard the bleat
Of the little grey snipe, so swift and fleet,
And I heard the plover that brings the rain,
Cry out in the dark again and again,
 Bolderogery! Bolderogery! Bolderogery-O!

Louder and louder the wind it blew,
   Bolderogery-rogery-O!
It gathered in sound as on it flew,
   Bolderogery-rogery-O!
And the Rogery birds cried in between
The gusts that gathered so swift and keen,
While the little black children out on the plain
Cried, 'Bird of the waters bring us the rain!'
   Bolderogery! Bolderogery! Bolderogery-O!

MARY GILMORE

'Bolderogery' is an Australian aborigine word meaning 'the rainbird' or 'the rain-bringer', and is the name given by the Waradgery tribe to the spur-winged plover. White people shortened it to 'Roger', or (for more than one) 'the Rogery birds'.

RAIN SONG

Hi-iya, naiho-o ! The earth is rumbling
From the beating of our basket drums.
The earth is rumbling from the beating
Of our basket drums, everywhere humming.
Earth is rumbling, everywhere raining.

Hi-iya, naiho-o! Pluck out the feathers
   From the wing of the eagle and turn them
Toward the east where lie the large clouds.
   Hi-iya, naiho-o! Pluck out the soft down
From the breast of the eagle and turn it
   Toward the west where sail the small clouds.
Hi-iya, naiho-o ! Beneath the abode
   Of the rain gods it is thundering;
Large corn is there. *Hi-iya, naiho-o!*
   Beneath the abode of the rain gods
It is raining; small corn is there.

PIMA INDIANS, NORTH AMERICA

This song was thought to produce rain. The feathers and down of the
eagle represent the gathering clouds.

PLAINT AGAINST THE FOG

Don't you ever,
You up in the sky,
Don't you ever get tired
Of having the clouds between you and us?

NOOTKA INDIANS, NORTH AMERICA

AZTEC SONG

we only came to sleep
we only came to dream
it is not true
no it is not true
that we came to live on the earth

we are changed into the grass of springtime
our hearts will grow green again
and they will open their petals
but our body is like a rose tree
 it puts forth flowers and then withers

NAHUATL INDIANS, MEXICO;
Translated by Lowell Dunham

THE SOLDIER CAMPION

For Ishbel, aged five

Campion so small and brave
Shaking in the Cornish wind
Guard the lady well whose arms
Are bright upon your shield.

When below your hill you see
The banners of an army come
Cry out with your little voice
And growl upon your little drum.

The ragged robin at your side
Shall your gallant sergeant be
And the elver in the pool
Your admiral upon the sea.

Campion red, upon your hill
Shaking in the Cornish gale,
Guard the lady for whose sake
I have written down this tale.

W. S. GRAHAM

elver : a young eel

TWO OR THREE POSIES

Two or three Posies
With two or three simples –
Two or three Noses
With two or three pimples –
Two or three wise men
And two or three ninny's –
Two or three purses
And two or three guineas –
Two or three raps
At two or three doors –
Two or three naps
Of two or three hours –
Two or three Cats
And two or three mice –
Two or three sprats
At a very great price –
Two or three sandies
And two or three tabbies –
Two or three dandies
And two Mrs –   mum!
Two or three Smiles
And two or three frowns –
Two or three Miles
To two or three towns –
Two or three pegs
For two or three bonnets –
Two or three dove eggs
To hatch into sonnets.

JOHN KEATS

simples : herbs used for making medicine

CARVE HER NAME

This is my tree. Carve her name
With a sharp knife, numb on my thumb.
The soft inch of bark opens gently,
Letter lips gape one by one;
Water runs over my arm.

Carve her name also, by me,
Cut shadow into the sun,
Her warm name open and growing.
Whichever way loving can turn
This tree wears us both on the bone.

MICHAEL BALDWIN

STRUTHILL WELL

Three white stones,
And three black pins,
Three yellow gowans
Off the green,

Into the well,
With a one, two, three,
And a fortune, a fortune,
Come to me.

ANONYMOUS, SCOTTISH

gowans: daisies

THIS IS A RUNE I HAVE HEARD
A TREE SAY

This is a rune I have heard a tree say:
'Love me. I cannot run away.'

This is a rune I have heard a lark cry:
'So high! But I cannot reach the sky.'

This is a rune I have heard a dog bark:
'I see what is not even there in the dark.'

This is a rune I have heard a fish weep:
'I am trying to find you when I leap.'

This is a rune I have heard a cat miaow:
'I died eight times so be kind to me now.'

This is a rune I have heard a man say:
'Hold your head up and you see far away.'

GEORGE BARKER

rune : a mysterious or magic saying, sometimes written in letters particularly suitable for carving on stone or wood

CHARMS AND SPELLS

THE SONG AT THE WELL

Enter COREBUS, *and* ZELANTO, *the foul Wench, to the well for water.*

COREBUS Come, my duck, come: I have now got a wife: thou art fair, art thou not?

ZELANTO My Corebus, the fairest alive; make no doubt of that.

COREBUS Come, wench, are we almost at the well?

ZELANTO Ay, Corebus, we are almost at the well now. I'll go fetch some water: sit down while I dip my pitcher in.

A Head comes up with ears of corn, and she combs them in her lap.

VOICE Gently dip, but not too deep,
    For fear you make the golden beard to weep.
    Fair maiden, white and red,
    Comb me smooth, and stroke my head,
    And thou shalt have some cockle-bread.

A Second Head comes up full of gold, which she combs into her lap.

SECOND HEAD Gently dip, but not too deep,
    For fear thou make the golden beard to weep.
    Fair maid, white and red,
    Comb me smooth, and stroke my head,
    And every hair a sheaf shall be,
    And every sheaf a golden tree.

GEORGE PEELE
From *The Old Wives' Tale*

Corebus has been blinded by Sacrapant the Conjurer, or enchanter. Cockle-bread was bread specially prepared and used as a love-charm. Some say that it was kneaded with the knees.

AMERGIN'S CHARM

I am a stag: *of seven tines,*
I am a flood: *across a plain,*
I am a wind: *on a deep lake,*
I am a tear: *the Sun lets fall,*
I am a hawk: *above the cliff,*
I am a thorn: *beneath the nail,*
I am a wonder: *among flowers,*
I am a wizard: *who but I*
Sets the cool head aflame with smoke?

I am a spear: *that roars for blood,*
I am a salmon: *in a pool,*
I am a lure: *from paradise,*
I am a hill: *where poets walk,*
I am a boar: *renowned and red,*
I am a breaker: *threatening doom,*
I am a tide: *that drags to death,*
I am an infant: *who but I*
Peeps from the unhewn dolmen arch?

I am the womb: *of every holt,*
I am the blaze: *on every hill,*
I am the queen: *of every hive,*
I am the shield: *for every head,*
I am the grave: *of every hope.*

ROBERT GRAVES
Restored from medieval Irish and Welsh variants

tine: the pointed branch of an antler
dolmen: form of prehistoric arch, consisting of two short stone uprights,
and one flat stone across the top

INVOCATION OF A POET SEEKING INSPIRATION

O Sun, thou art reborn out of darkness;
Thou comest out of deep places, thou comest out of the
  terrible shadows;
Thou wast dead, thou art alive again.
O Sun, behold me, help me:
The word of power died in my heart,
Let it be reborn again as thou,
Let it fill me with light as thou,
Let it soar above the shadows,
Let it live!
So shall I be eloquent.

FROM THE GILBERT ISLANDS, MICRONESIA

ON A MIDSUMMER EVE

I idly cut a parsley stalk,
And blew therein towards the moon;
I had not thought what ghosts would walk
With shivering footsteps to my tune.

I went, and knelt, and scooped my hand
As if to drink, into the brook,
And a faint figure seemed to stand
Above me, with the bygone look.

I lipped rough rhymes of chance, not choice,
I thought not what my words might be;
There came into my ear a voice
That turned a tenderer verse for me.

THOMAS HARDY

THE NIGHT-PIECE, TO JULIA

Her Eyes the Glow-worme lend thee,
The Shooting Starres attend thee;
   And the Elves also,
   Whose little eyes glow,
Like the sparks of fire, befriend thee.

No *Will-o'-th'-Wispe* mis-light thee;
Nor Snake, or Slow-worme bite thee:
   But on, on thy way
   Not making a stay,
Since Ghost ther's none to affright thee.

Let not the darke thee cumber;
What though the Moon do's slumber?
   The Starres of the night
   Will lend thee their light,
Like Tapers cleare without number.

Then *Julia* let me wooe thee,
Thus, thus to come unto me:
   And when I shall meet
   Thy silv'ry feet,
My soule Ile poure into thee.

ROBERT HERRICK

SPELL OF CREATION

Within the flower there lies a seed,
Within the seed there springs a tree,
Within the tree there spreads a wood.

In the wood there burns a fire,
And in the fire there melts a stone,
Within the stone a ring of iron.

Within the ring there lies an O
Within the O there looks an eye,
In the eye there swims a sea,

And in the sea reflected sky,
And in the sky there shines the sun,
Within the sun a bird of gold.

Within the bird there beats a heart,
And from the heart there flows a song,
And in the song there sings a word.

In the word there speaks a world,
A word of joy, a world of grief,
From joy and grief there springs my love.

Oh love, my love, there springs a world,
And on the world there shines a sun
And in the sun there burns a fire,

Within the fire consumes my heart
And in my heart there beats a bird,
And in the bird there wakes an eye,

Within the eye, earth, sea and sky,
Earth, sky and sea within an O
Lie like the seed within the flower.

KATHLEEN RAINE

AN INVOCATION

Hear, sweet Spirit, hear the spell,
Lest a blacker charm compel!
So shall the midnight breezes swell
With thy deep long-lingering knell.

And at evening evermore,
In a chapel on the shore,
Shall the chaunter, sad and saintly,
Yellow tapers burning faintly,
Doleful masses chaunt for thee,
    Miserere Domine!

Hush! the cadence dies away
On the quiet moonlight sea:
The boatmen rest their oars and say,
    Miserere Domine!

SAMUEL TAYLOR COLERIDGE
From *Remorse*

THE FAERY BEAM UPON YOU

The faery beam upon you,
The stars to glister on you;
  A Moon of light,
  In the Noon of night,
Till the Fire-drake hath o'er-gone you.

The Wheel of Fortune guide you,
The Boy with the Bow beside you,
  Run aye in the way,
  Till the Bird of day,
And the luckier lot betide you.

BEN JONSON
From *The Gypsies Metamorphos'd*

Fire-drake : fiery dragon or meteor

UPON THAT NIGHT, WHEN FAIRIES LIGHT

Upon that night, when Fairies light,
  On Cassilis Downans dance,
Or owre the lays, in splendid blaze,
  On sprightly coursers prance;
Or for Colean the route is ta'en,
  Beneath the moon's pale beams;
There, up the Cove, to stray an' rove
  Amang the rocks an' streams
          To sport that night.

Amang the bony, winding banks,
  Where Doon rins, wimplin, clear,
Where Bruce ance rul'd the martial ranks
  An' shook his Carrick spear,
Some merry, friendly, country-folks
  Together did convene,
To burn their nits, an' pou their stocks,
  An' haud their Halloween
          Fu' blythe that night . . .

The auld Guidwife's weel-hoordet nits
  Are round an' round divided,
An' monie lads' and lasses' fates
  Are there that night decided:
Some kindle, couthie, side by side,
  An' burn thegither trimly;
Some start awa, wi' saucy pride,
  And jump out-owre the chimlie
          Fu' high that night.

Jean slips in twa wi' tentie e'e;
  Wha 'twas, she wadna tell;
But this is *Jock*, an' this *me*,
  She says in to hersel:
He bleez'd owre her, an' she owre him,
  As they wad never màir part,
Till fuff! he started up the lum,
  An' Jean had e'en a sàir heart
        To see't that night.

ROBERT BURNS
From *Halloween*

lays: fields, pastures
wimplin: meandering, wandering
nits: nuts
pou their stocks: pulling cabbage plants or kale, as a Halloween game.
From the type pulled (big, small, straight or crooked, etc.), the future was
foretold
haud: hold
couthie: kind, agreeable, loving
thegither: together
chimlie: fireplace
tentie: careful
bleez'd: blazed
lum: chimney

SPELLS

I dance and dance without any feet –
This is the spell of the ripening wheat.

With never a tongue I've a tale to tell –
This is the meadow-grasses' spell.

I give you health without any fee –
This is the spell of the apple-tree.

I rhyme and riddle without any book –
This is the spell of the bubbling brook.

Without any legs I run for ever –
This is the spell of the mighty river.

I fall for ever and not at all –
This is the spell of the waterfall.

Without a voice I roar aloud –
This is the spell of the thunder-cloud.

No button or seam has my white coat –
This is the spell of the leaping goat.

I can cheat strangers with never a word –
This is the spell of the cuckoo-bird.

We have tongues in plenty but speak no names –
This is the spell of the fiery flames.

The creaking door has a spell to riddle –
I play a tune without any fiddle.

JAMES REEVES

WHITE WITCHCRAFT

If you and I could change to beasts, what
    beast should either be?
Shall you and I play Jove for once? Turn
    fox then, I decree!
Shy wild sweet stealer of the grapes! Now
    do your worst on me!

And thus you think to spite your friend –
    turned loathsome? What, a toad?
So, all men shrink and shun me! Dear men,
    pursue your road!
Leave but my crevice in the stone, a reptile's
    fit abode!

Now say your worst, Canidia! 'He's
    loathsome, I allow:
There may or may not lurk a pearl beneath
    his puckered brow:
But see his eyes that follow mine – love
    lasts there anyhow.'

ROBERT BROWNING

54

THE CHARM

Uisge cloiche gan irraidh

Water, I did not seek you,
Water of hollow stone;
I crossed no one's acre to find you –
You were where my geese lie down.

I dip my fingers and sprinkle,
While three times over I say,
'Chance-bound and chance-found water
Can take a numbness away.'

The numbness that leaves me vacant
Of thought and will and deed
Like the moveless clock that I gaze on –
It will go where the ravens breed.

I empty the stone; on the morrow
I shall rise with spirit alive;
Gallant amongst the gallant,
I shall speak and lead and strive.

In search there is no warrant,
By chance is the charm shown:
Water, I did not seek you,
Water of hollow stone!

PADRAIC COLUM

The Irish words mean 'water from an unsought stone'.

CURSES

A SPELL TO DESTROY LIFE

Listen!
    Now I have come to step over your soul
        (I know your clan)
        (I know your name)
        (I have stolen your spit and buried it under earth)
    I bury your soul under earth
    I cover you over with black rock
    I cover you over with black cloth
    I cover you over with black slabs
    You disappear forever

    Your path leads to the
            Black Coffin
            in the hills of the Darkening Land

    So let it be for you

    The clay of the hills covers you
    The black clay of the Darkening Land

    Your soul fades away

    It becomes blue (colour of despair)
    When darkness comes your spirit shrivels and
        dwindles to disappear forever
Listen!

            CHEROKEE INDIANS, NORTH AMERICA

ST NEWLINA'S STAFF

This fig tree is her staff, folks say.
Destroy it not in any way.
Upon it lays a dreadful curse,
Who plucks a leaf will need a hearse.

ANONYMOUS

Before being destroyed in a gale, a fig tree once grew from the wall
at St Newlyn Church near Newquay in Cornwall. Whoever took a leaf or a
fig from it was said to die within a year.

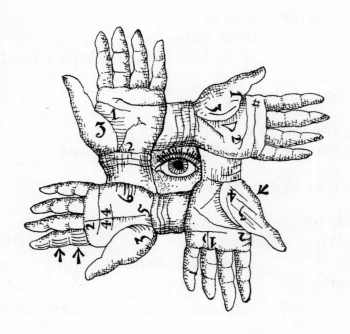

CHARM FOR STRIKING FEAR INTO A TIGER AND HARDENING ONE'S OWN HEART

O Earth-Shaker, rumble and quake!
Let iron needles be my body-hairs,
Let copper needles be my body-hairs!
Let poisonous snakes be my beard,
A crocodile my tongue,
And a roaring tiger in the dimple of my chin.
Be my voice the trumpet of an elephant,
Yes, like the roar of the thunderbolt.
May your lips be fast closed and your teeth clenched;
And not till the heavens and the earth are moved
May your heart be moved
To be angry with me or to seek to destroy me . . .
Let splendour reside in my person.
Whoever talks of encountering me,
A cunning lion shall be his opponent.
O all things that have life,
Endure not to confront my gaze!
It is I who shall confront the gaze of you,
By the virtue of 'There is no god but God.'

FROM THE MALAY PENINSULA

GLAUCOPIS

John Fane Dingle
  By Rumney Brook
Shot a crop-eared owl,
  For pigeon mistook:

Caught her by the lax wing.
  – She, as she dies,
Thrills his warm soul through
  With her deep eyes.

Corpse-eyes are eerie:
  Tiger-eyes fierce:
John Fane Dingle found
  Owl-eyes worse.

Owl-eyes on night-clouds,
  Constant as Fate:
Owl-eyes in baby's face:
  On dish and plate:

Owl-eyes, without sound.
  – Pale of hue
John died of no complaint,
  With owl-eyes too.

RICHARD HUGHES

LONG JOHN BROWN & LITTLE
MARY BELL

Little Mary Bell had a Fairy in a Nut,
Long John Brown had the Devil in his Gut:
Long John Brown lov'd Little Mary Bell,
And the Fairy drew the Devil into the Nut-shell.

Her Fairy Skip'd out & her Fairy Skip'd in;
He laugh'd at the Devil saying 'Love is a Sin.'
The Devil he raged & the Devil he was wroth,
And the Devil enter'd into the Young Man's broth.

He was soon in the Gut of the loving Young Swain,
For John eat & drank to drive away Love's pain;
But all he could do he grew thinner & thinner,
Tho' he eat & drank as much as ten Men for his dinner.

Some said he had a Wolf in his stomach day & night,
Some said he had the Devil & they guess'd right;
The Fairy skip'd about in his Glory, Joy & Pride,
And he laugh'd at the Devil till poor John Brown died.

Then the Fairy skip'd out of the old Nut-shell,
And woe & alack for Pretty Mary Bell!
For the Devil crept in when the Fairy skip'd out,
And there goes Miss Bell with her fusty old Nut.

WILLIAM BLAKE

HER STRONG ENCHANTMENTS
FAILING

Her strong enchantments failing,
Her towers of fear in wreck,
Her limbecks dried of poisons
And the knife at her neck,

The Queen of air and darkness
Begins to shrill and cry,
'O young man, O my slayer,
To-morrow you shall die.'

O Queen of air and darkness,
I think 'tis truth you say,
And I shall die to-morrow;
But you will die to-day.

A. E. HOUSMAN

limbeck or alembic : piece of apparatus used for distilling by alchemists, or
medieval chemists

LA BELLE DAME SANS MERCI

O, what can ail thee, knight-at-arms,
Alone and palely loitering?
The sedge has wither'd from the lake,
And no birds sing.

O, what can ail thee, knight-at-arms,
So haggard and so woe-begone?
The squirrel's granary is full,
And the harvest's done.

I see a lilly on thy brow,
   With anguish moist and fever dew;
And on thy cheeks a fading rose
   Fast withereth too.

I met a lady in the meads,
   Full beautiful – a faery's child,
Her hair was long, her foot was light,
   And her eyes were wild.

I made a garland for her head,
   And bracelets too, and fragrant zone;
She look'd at me as she did love,
   And made sweet moan.

I set her on my pacing steed,
   And nothing else saw all day long;
For sidelong would she bend, and sing
   A faery's song.

She found me roots of relish sweet,
   And honey wild, and manna dew,
And sure in language strange she said –
   'I love thee true'.

She took me to her elfin grot,
   And there she wept and sigh'd full sore,
And there I shut her wild wild eyes
   With kisses four.

And there she lulled me asleep
   And there I dream'd – Ah! woe betide!
The latest dream I ever dream'd
   On the cold hill side.

I saw pale kings and princes too,
    Pale warriors, death-pale were they all;
They cried – 'La Belle Dame sans Merci
    Hath thee in thrall!'

I saw their starved lips in the gloam,
    With horrid warning gaped wide,
And I awoke and found me here,
    On the cold hill's side.

And this is why I sojourn here
    Alone and palely loitering,
Though the sedge has wither'd from the lake,
    And no birds sing.

JOHN KEATS

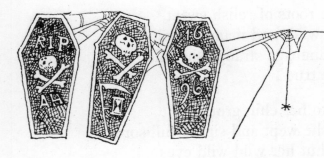

THE MAN IN THE WILDERNESS

The Man in the Wilderness asked of me
'How many blackberries grow in the sea?'
I answered him as I thought good,
'As many red herrings as grow in the wood.'

The Man in the Wilderness asked me why
His hen could swim, and his pig could fly.
I answered him briskly as I thought best,
'Because they were born in a cuckoo's nest.'

The Man in the Wilderness asked me to tell
The sands in the sea and I counted them well.
Says he with a grin, 'And not one more?'
I answered him bravely, 'You go and make sure!'

ANONYMOUS

It was once thought that with this chant, an evil spirit could be banished
to the Red Sea.

THERE SHE WEAVES BY NIGHT AND DAY

There she weaves by night and day
A magic web with colours gay.
She has heard a whisper say,
A curse is on her if she stay
            To look down to Camelot.
She knows not what the curse may be,
And so she weaveth steadily,
And little other care hath she,
            The Lady of Shalott.

And moving thro' a mirror clear
That hangs before her all the year,
Shadows of the world appear.
There she sees the highway near
      Winding down to Camelot:
There the river eddy whirls,
And there the surly village-churls,
And the red cloaks of market girls,
      Pass onward from Shalott.

Sometimes a troop of damsels glad,
An abbot on an ambling pad,
Sometimes a curly shepherd-lad,
Or long-hair'd page in crimson clad,
      Goes by to tower'd Camelot;
And sometimes thro' the mirror blue
The knights come riding two and two:
She hath no loyal knight and true,
      The Lady of Shalott.

But in her web she still delights
To weave the mirror's magic sights,
For often thro' the silent nights
A funeral, with plumes and lights,
      And music, went to Camelot:
Or when the moon was overhead,
Came two young lovers lately wed;
'I am half sick of shadows,' said
      The Lady of Shalott.

ALFRED, LORD TENNYSON
From *The Lady of Shalott*

pad: a soft saddle

NOBLE SISTERS

'Now did you mark a falcon,
    Sister dear, sister dear,
Flying toward my window
    In the morning cool and clear?
With jingling bells about her neck,
    But what beneath her wing?
It may have been a ribbon,
    Or it may have been a ring.' –
        'I marked a falcon swooping
            At the break of day:
        And for your love, my sister dove,
            I 'frayed the thief away.' –

'Or did you spy a ruddy hound,
    Sister fair and tall,
Went snuffing round my garden bound,
    Or crouched by my bower wall?
With a silken leash about his neck;
    But in his mouth may be
A chain of gold and silver links,
    Or a letter writ to me.' –
        'I heard a hound, highborn sister,
            Stood baying at the moon:
        I rose and drove him from your wall
            Lest you should wake too soon.' –

'Or did you meet a pretty page
    Sat swinging on the gate;
Sat whistling whistling like a bird,
    Or may be slept too late:
With eaglets broidered on his cap,
    And eaglets on his glove?

69

If you had turned his pockets out,
　You had found some pledge of love.' –
　　　'I met him at this daybreak,
　　　　Scarce the east was red:
　　　Lest the creaking gate should anger you,
　　　　I packed him home to bed.' –

'Oh patience sister. Did you see
　A young man tall and strong,
Swift-footed to uphold the right
And to uproot the wrong,
Come home across the desolate sea
　To woo me for his wife?
And in his heart my heart is locked,
　And in his life my life.' –
　　　'I met a nameless man, sister,
　　　　Hard by your chamber door:
　　　I said: Her husband loves her much.
　　　　And yet she loves him more.' –

'Fie, sister, fie, a wicked lie,
　A lie, a wicked lie,
I have none other love but him,
　Nor will have till I die.
And you have turned him from our door,
　And stabbed him with a lie:
I will go seek him thro' the world
　In sorrow till I die.' –
　　　'Go seek in sorrow, sister,
　　　　And find in sorrow too:
　　　If thus you shame our father's name
　　　　My curse go forth with you.'

CHRISTINA ROSSETTI

Warlocks
Witches
& Wizards

THE EGG-SHELL

The wind took off with the sunset –
The fog came up with the tide,
When the Witch of the North took an Egg-shell
With a little Blue Devil inside.
'Sink,' she said, 'or swim,' she said,
'It's all you will get from me.
And that is the finish of *him*!' she said,
And the Egg-shell went to sea.

The wind fell dead with the midnight –
The fog shut down like a sheet,
When the Witch of the North heard the Egg-shell
Feeling by hand for a fleet.
'Get!' she said, 'or you're gone,' she said,
But the little Blue Devil said 'No!'
'The sights are just coming on,' he said,
And he let the Whitehead go.

The wind got up with the morning –
The fog blew off with the rain,
When the Witch of the North saw the Egg-shell
And the little Blue Devil again.
'Did you swim?' she said. 'Did you sink?' she said,
And the little Blue Devil replied:
'For myself I swam, but I *think*,' he said,
'There's somebody sinking outside.'

RUDYARD KIPLING

HALLOWE'EN

This is the night when witches fly
On their whizzing broomsticks through the wintry sky;
Steering up the pathway where the stars are strewn,
They stretch skinny fingers to the waking moon.

This is the night when old wives tell
Strange and creepy stories, tales of charm and spell;
Peering at the pictures flaming in the fire
They wait for whispers from a ghostly choir.

This is the night when angels go
In and out the houses, winging o'er the snow;
Clearing out the demons from the countryside
They make it new and ready for Christmastide.

LEONARD CLARK

ALL HAIL, GREAT MASTER!

Ariel   All hail, great master! grave sir, hail! I come
To answer thy best pleasure; be't to fly,
To swim, to dive into the fire, to ride
On the curl'd clouds: to thy strong bidding task
Ariel and all his quality.
   Prospero   Hast thou, spirit,
Perform'd to point the tempest that I bade thee?
   Ariel   To every article.
I boarded the king's ship; now on the beak,
Now in the waist, the deck, in every cabin,
I flam'd amazement: sometime I'd divide
And burn in many places; on the topmast,
The yards, and boresprit, would I flame distinctly,
Then meet, and join: Jove's lightnings, the precursors
O' the dreadful thunder-claps, more momentary
And sight-outrunning were not: the fire and cracks
Of sulphurous roaring the most might Neptune
Seem to besiege and make his bold waves tremble,
Yea, his dread trident shake.

WILLIAM SHAKESPEARE
From The Tempest

THE WARDEN

To the tune of: 'They played in the beautiful garden . . .'

They played in the beautiful garden
Those children of high degree,
But she sighed as she swam with the Warden
In the depths of the Zuyder Zee.

Oh why did you take me away
From the children I loved so well?
I had other plans in my heart, dear
For the child of my latest spell.

The Warden has decked her with seaweed,
And shells of an ancient design,
But she sighs as she presses his fingers,
My heart can never be thine.

He sits in the golden chair
With the child he would call his own,
But the beautiful child has expired,
He nurses a sea-green stone.

STEVIE SMITH

THE WITCH

Weary went the old Witch,
Weary of her pack,
She sat her down by the churchyard wall,
And jerked it off her back.

The cord brake, yes, the cord brake,
Just where the dead did lie,
And Charms and Spells and Sorceries
Spilled out beneath the sky.

Weary was the old Witch;
She rested her old eyes
From the lantern-fruited yew trees,
And the scarlet of the skies;

And out the dead came stumbling,
From every rift and crack,
Silent as moss, and plundered
The gaping pack.

They wish them, three times over,
Away they skip full soon:
Bat and Mole and Leveret,
Under the rising moon;

Owl and Newt and Nightjar:
They take their shapes and creep
Silent as churchyard lichen,
While she squats asleep.

All of these dead were stirring:
Each unto each did call,
'A Witch, a Witch is sleeping
Under the churchyard wall;

'A Witch, a Witch is sleeping . . .'
The shrillness ebbed away;
And up the way-worn moon clomb bright,
Hard on the track of day.

She shone, high, wan, and silvery;
Day's colours paled and died:
And, save the mute and creeping worm,
Nought else was there beside.

Names may be writ; and mounds rise;
Purporting, Here be bones:
But empty is that churchyard
Of all save stones.

Owl and Newt and Nightjar,
Leveret, Bat, and Mole
Haunt and call in the twilight
Where she slept, poor soul.

WALTER DE LA MARE

WHEN SHALL WE THREE MEET
AGAIN

First Witch   When shall we three meet again
In thunder, lightning, or in rain?
Second Witch   When the hurlyburly's done,
When the battle's lost and won.
Third Witch   That will be ere the set of sun.
First Witch   Where the place?
Second Witch   Upon the heath.
Third Witch   There to meet with Macbeth.
First Witch   I come, Graymalkin!
Second Witch   Paddock calls.
Third Witch   Anon.
All   Fair is foul, and foul is fair:
Hover through the fog and filthy air.

WILLIAM SHAKESPEARE
From *Macbeth*

Graymalkin: the witch's cat
Paddock: a toad or frog

DAME HICKORY

'Dame Hickory, Dame Hickory,
Here's sticks for your fire,
Furze-twigs, and oak-twigs,
And beech-twigs, and briar!'
But when old Dame Hickory came for to sée,
She found 'twas the voice of the False Faërie.

'Dame Hickory, Dame Hickory,
Here's meat for your broth,
Goose-flesh, and hare's flesh,
And pig's trotters both!'
But when old Dame Hickory came for to see,
She found 'twas the voice of the False Faërie.

'Dame Hickory, Dame Hickory,
Here's a wolf at your door,
His teeth grinning white,
And his tongue wagging sore!'
'Nay!' said Dame Hickory, 'ye False Faërie!'
But a wolf 'twas indeed, and famished was he.

'Dame Hickory, Dame Hickory,
Here's buds for your tomb,
Bramble, and lavender,
And rosemary bloom!'
'Whsst!' sighs Dame Hickory, 'you False Faërie,
You cry like a wolf, you do, and trouble poor me.'

WALTER DE LA MARE

THRICE THE BRINDED CAT HATH
MEW'D

First Witch   Thrice the brinded cat hath mew'd.
Second Witch   Thrice, and once the hedge-pig whin'd.
Third Witch   Harpier cries: 'Tis time, 'tis time.
First Witch   Round about the cauldron go;
   In the poison'd entrails throw.
   Toad, that under cold stone
   Days and nights hast thirty-one
   Swelter'd venom sleeping got,
   Boil thou first i' the charmed pot.
All   Double, double toil and trouble;
   Fire, burn; and, cauldron, bubble.
Second Witch   Fillet of a fenny snake,
   In the cauldron boil and bake;
   Eye of newt, and toe of frog,
   Wool of bat, and tongue of dog,
   Adder's fork, and blind-worms' sting,
   Lizard's leg, and howlet's wing,
   For a charm of powerful trouble;
   Like a hell-broth boil and bubble.
All   Double, double toil and trouble,
   Fire, burn; and, cauldron, bubble.
Third Witch   Scale of dragon, tooth of wolf,
   Witches' mummy, maw and gulf
   Of the ravin'd salt-sea shark,
   Root of hemlock digg'd i' the dark,
   Liver of blaspheming Jew,

brinded : tabby
Harpier ; familiar spirit, or demon under her power; harpy; a fabulous
creature with a woman's body and a bird's wings and claws
fenny : from a fen or swamp

Gall of goat, and slips of yew
Sliver'd in the moon's eclipse,
Nose of Turk, and Tartar's lips,
Finger of birth-strangled babe
Ditch-deliver'd by a drab,
Make the gruel thick and slab:
Add thereto a tiger's chaudron,
For the ingredients of our cauldron.
All   Double, double toil and trouble;
   Fire, burn; and, cauldron, bubble.
Second Witch   Cool it with a baboon's blood,
   Then the charm is firm and good.

WILLIAM SHAKESPEARE
From *Macbeth*

chaudron : entrails

THE HAGS' SONG

1 Hag

I have been all day looking after
A raven feeding upon a quarter;
And, soon as she turn'd her beak to the south,
I snatch'd this morsel out of her mouth.

2 Hag

I have been gathering wolves' hairs,
The mad dogs' foams, and adders' ears;
The spurging of a deadman's eyes:
And all since the evening star did rise.

3 Hag

I last night lay all alone
O' the ground, to hear the mandrake groan;

And pluck'd him up, though he grew full low:
And, as I had done, the cock did crow.

4 Hag

And I ha' been choosing out this skull
From charnel houses that were full;
From private grots and public pits;
And frighted a sexton out of his wits.

5 Hag

Under a cradle I did creep
By day; and when the child was asleep
At night, I suck'd the breath; and rose,
And pluck'd the nodding nurse by the nose.

6 Hag

I had a dagger: what did I with that?
Killed an infant to have his fat.
A piper it got at a church-ale,
I bade him again blow wind i' the tail.

7 Hag

A murderer, yonder, was hung in chains;
The sun and the wind had shrunk his veins:
I bit off a sinew; I clipp'd his hair;
I brought off his rags, that danc'd i' the air.

8 Hag

The scritch-owl's eggs and the feathers black,
The blood of the frog, and the bone in his back

spurging : frothing
mandrake : the mandrake or mandragora was thought to be a magic plant,
and its root to give a shriek when pulled out of the earth

I have been getting; and made of his skin
A purset, to keep sir Cranion in.

9 Hag

And I ha' been plucking (plants among)
Hemlock, henbane, adder's tongue,
Night-shade, moon-wort, libbard's-bane;
And twice by the dogs was like to be ta'en.

10 Hag

I from the jaws of a gardener's bitch
Did snatch these bones, and then leap'd the ditch:
Yet went I back to the house again,
Kill'd the black cat, and here is the brain.

11 Hag

I went to the toad, breeds under the wall,
I charmed him out, and he came at my call;
I scratch'd out the eyes of the owl before;
I tore the bat's wing: what would you have more?

Dame

Yes: I have brought to help your vows,
Horned poppy, cypress boughs,
The fig-tree wild, that grows on tombs,
And juice, that from the larch-tree comes,
  The basilisk's blood, and the viper's skin:
  And now our orgies let's begin.

BEN JONSON
From *The Masque of Queens*

Cranion: a skull
libbard's-bane: wolf's-bane, a herb. Mixed with meat it was thought to
be a wolf-poison
Dame: Ate, the Greek goddess of vengeance and mischief

OH! MY NAME IS
JOHN WELLINGTON WELLS

Oh! my name is John Wellington Wells –
I'm a dealer in magic and spells,
   In blessings and curses,
   And ever-filled purses,
In prophecies, witches, and knells!
If you want a proud foe to 'make tracks' –
If you'd melt a rich uncle in wax –
   You've but to look in
   On our resident Djinn,
Number seventy, Simmery Axe.

We've a first-class assortment of magic;
   And for raising a posthumous shade
With effects that are comic or tragic,
   There's no cheaper house in the trade.
Love-philtre – we've quantities of it;
   And for knowledge if any one burns,
We keep an extremely small prophet, a prophet
   Who brings us unbounded returns:
     For he can prophesy
     With a wink *of* his eye,
     Peep with security
     Into futurity,
     Sum up your history,
     Clear up a mystery,
     Humour proclivity
     For a nativity.

With mirrors so magical,
Tetrapods tragical,
Bogies spectacular,
Answers oracular,
Facts astronomical,
Solemn or comical,
And, if you want it, he
Makes a reduction on taking a quantity!
    Oh!
If any one anything lacks,
He'll find it all ready in stacks,
    If he'll only look in
    On the resident Djinn,
Number seventy, Simmery Axe!

W. S. GILBERT
From *The Sorcerer*

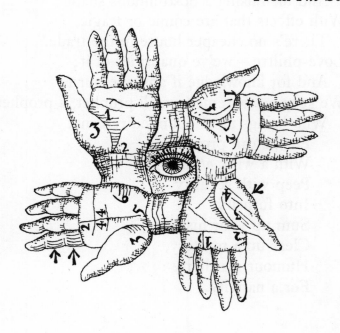

THE GREAT NEMO

The gypsy, the Great Nemo,
  Palmist, Clairvoyant and Occultist,
Spent his days on the rusty pier in a haunted cabin
Clamped like a barnacle to the ironwork,
Vibrant to the swing and rhythm of great seas.
His magician's cave was full of cheap jewellery and china
  vases
To be bought for the law's sake at exorbitant prices.
When the door opened,
Old, brown newspaper cuttings, portraying the Great
  Nemo
Fortune-telling at fêtes for charity,
Flapped and wriggled flatly from the walls.

His cabin, though full of shadows, was not dark:
By the man's own future it was haunted.
Sea-light poured in at a round window like a port-hole,
Illuminating the upper part
Of his short, thick-set body, sitting at the table,
And spot-lighting every wrinkle, every line on the
  coconut-coloured face,
Causing the flat gypsy glare of his eyes
To flare with an animal light, as they turned, burning,
Toward the crystal on the table.

'You are very intuitive,' the Great Nemo would say,
'Your husband doesn't understand you.
    You would make your fortune on the stage.'
That did not tire him.
But when he threw back his client's fat hand,
And for an extra half-crown concentrated on the crystal,
Then he became an ancestral voice,
Prophesying from a caravan in distant countries.

OSBERT SITWELL

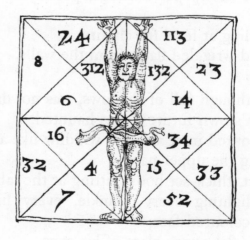

CHANGELINGS

HAPLESS

Hapless, hapless, I must be
All the hours of life I see,
Since my foolish nurse did once
Bed me on her leggen bones;
Since my mother did not weel
To snip my nails with blades of steel.
Had they laid me on a pillow
In a cot of water willow,
Had they bitten finger and thumb,
Not to such ill hap I had come.

WALTER DE LA MARE

THE STOLEN CHILD

Where dips the rocky highland
Of Sleuth Wood in the lake,
There lies a leafy island
Where flapping herons wake
The drowsy water-rats;
There we've hid our faery vats,
Full of berries
And of reddest stolen cherries.
Come away, O human child!
To the waters and the wild
With a faery, hand in hand,
For the world's more full of weeping than you can
*   understand.*

Where the wave of moonlight glosses
The dim grey sands with light,
Far off by furthest Rosses
We foot it all the night,
Weaving olden dances,
Mingling hands and mingling glances
Till the moon has taken flight;
To and fro we leap
And chase the froth bubbles,
While the world is full of troubles
And is anxious in its sleep.
Come away, O human child!
To the waters and the wild
With a faery, hand in hand,
For the world's more full of weeping than you can
*   understand.*

Where the wandering water gushes
From the hills above Glen-Car,
In pools among the rushes
That scarce could bathe a star,
We seek for slumbering trout
And whispering in their ears
Give them unquiet dreams;
Leaning softly out
From ferns that drop their tears
Over the young streams.
Come away, O human child!
To the waters and the wild
With a faery, hand in hand,
For the world's more full of weeping than you can
    understand.

Away with us he's going,
The solemn-eyed:
He'll hear no more the lowing
Of the calves on the warm hillside
Or the kettle on the hob
Sing peace into his breast,
Or see the brown mice bob
Round and round the oatmeal-chest.
For he comes, the human child,
To the waters and the wild
With a faery, hand in hand,
From a world more full of weeping than he can
    understand.

                                        W. B. YEATS

THE THREE BEGGARS

'Twas autumn daybreak gold and wild
   While past St Ann's grey tower they shuffled
Three beggars spied a fairy-child
   In crimson mantle muffled.

The daybreak lighted up her face
   All pink, and sharp, and emerald-eyed;
She looked on them a little space,
   And shrill as hautboy cried: –

'O three tall footsore men in rags
   Which walking this gold morn I see,
What will ye give me from your bags
   For fairy kisses three?'

The first, that was a reddish man,
   Out of his bundle takes a crust:
'La, by the tombstones of St Ann
   There's fee, if fee ye must!'

The second, that was a chestnut man,
   Out of his bundle draws a bone:
'La, by the belfry of St Ann,
   And all my breakfast gone!'

The third, that was a yellow man,
   Out of his bundle picks a groat,
'La, by the Angel of St Ann,
   And I must go without.'

That changeling, lean and icy-lipped,
    Touched crust, and bone, and groat, and lo!
Beneath her finger taper-tipped
    The magic all ran through.

Instead of crust a peacock pie,
    Instead of bone sweet venison,
Instead of groat a white lily
    With seven blooms thereon.

And each fair cup was deep with wine:
    Such was the changeling's charity
The sweet feast was enough for nine,
    But not too much for three.

O toothsome meat in jelly froze!
    O tender haunch of elfin stag!
Oh, rich the odour that arose!
    Oh, plump with scraps each bag!

There, in the daybreak gold and wild,
    Each merry-hearted beggar man
Drank deep unto the fairy child,
    And blessed the good St Ann.

WALTER DE LA MARE

THE CHANGELING

Mary's mother is tall and fair,
Her father is freckled with ginger hair,
And they live in a house all polished and neat
In the very centre of Riverside Street.

But Mary is dark and thin and wild,
And she doesn't laugh like a human child,
And she doesn't cry like you and me
With tears as salt as the brooding sea.

For when Mary giggles the rattling sound
Is worse than the traffic for miles around;
And the sobs that heave Mary's shoulders high,
Leave her throat parched and her wide eyes dry.

In the classroom Mary works on her own,
And she plays in the playground quite alone.
In church she will not pray or sing,
For she never will join in anything.

It can only be that ten years ago,
In hurtling sleet and blinding snow,
Some dreaming wizards or spiteful elves
Went cradle-swapping to please themselves,

Took the real Mary to join their race
And left their fledgling, in her place,
To grow both beautiful and sly
With power to destroy in her evil eye.

CHANGELINGS

And the only thing both Marys share
Is that they are homesick everywhere.
So sumptiously by the fairies fed,
The one is hungry for human bread.

The other however the heat's turned higher
Is cold for the lack of fairy fire.
And the parents cannot know what is meant
By their daughter's waspish discontent.

Her sulks and tempers are never done,
She's a stock of harsh words for everyone;
While they, dismayed by their puzzling fate,
Go to bed early and get up late.

So now the mother is bent and grey,
And the father sits in his chair all day,
And Riverside Street cannot abide
The slum that their house has become inside.

SHIRLEY TOULSON

ghosts
and hauntings

SONG OF TWO GHOSTS

My friend
This is a wide world
We're travelling over
Walking on the moonlight.

INDIAN SONG FROM OMAHA,
NORTH AMERICA

OLD MOTHER LAIDINWOOL

Old Mother Laidinwool had nigh twelve months been
dead.
She heard the hops was doing well, an' so popped up her
head,
For said she: 'The lads I've picked with when I was
young and fair,
They're bound to be at hopping and I'm bound to meet
'em there!'
　　Let me up and go
　　Back to the work I know, Lord!
　　Back to the work I know, Lord!
　　For it's dark where I lie down, My Lord!
　　An' it's dark where I lie down!

Old Mother Laidinwool, she give her bones a shake,
An' trotted down the churchyard-path as fast as she
could make.
She met the Parson walking, but she says to him, says
she: —
'Oh don't let no one trouble for a poor old ghost like me!'

'Twas all a warm September an' the hops had flourished
    grand.
She saw the folks get into 'em with stockin's on their
    hands;
An' none of 'em was foreigners but all which she had
    known,
And old Mother Laidinwool she blessed 'em every one.

She saw her daughters picking an' their childern them-
    beside,
An' she moved among the babies an' she stilled 'em
    when they cried.
She saw their clothes was bought, not begged, an' they
    was clean an' fat,
An' Old Mother Laidinwool she thanked the Lord for that.

Old Mother Laidinwool she waited on all day
Until it come too dark to see an' people went away –
Until it come too dark to see an' lights began to show,
An' old Mother Laidinwool she hadn't where to go.

Old Mother Laidinwool she give her bones a shake,
An' trotted back to churchyard-mould as fast as she
    could make.
She went where she was bidden to an' there laid down
    her ghost, . . .
An' the Lord have mercy on you in the Day you need it
    most!
      Let me in again,
      Out of the wet an' rain, Lord!
      Out of the wet an' rain, Lord!
      For it's best as You shall say, My Lord!
      An' it's best as You shall say!

RUDYARD KIPLING

THE STRANGE VISITOR

A wife was sitting at her reel ae nicht;
And aye she sat, and aye she reeled, and aye she wished
    for company.

In cam a pair o braid, braid soles, and sat down at the
    fireside;
And aye she sat, and aye she reeled, and aye she wished
    for company.

In cam a pair o sma, sma legs, and sat down on the braid,
    braid soles;
And aye she sat, and aye she reeled, and aye she wished
    for company.

In cam a pair o sma, sma thees, and sat down on the
    sma, sma legs;
And aye she sat, and aye she reeled, and aye she wished
    for company.

In cam a pair o muckle, muckle hips, and sat down on
    the sma, sma thees;
And aye she sat, and aye she reeled, and aye she wished
    for company.

In cam a sma, sma waist, and sat down on the muckle
    muckle hips;
And aye she sat, and aye she reeled, and aye she wished
    for company.

In cam a pair o braid, braid shouthers, and sat down on
    the sma, sma waist;
And aye she sat, and aye she reeled, and aye she wished
    for company.

thees: thighs

In cam a pair o sma, sma arms, and sat down on the
  braid, braid shouthers;
And aye she sat, and aye she reeled, and aye she wished
  for company.

In cam a pair o muckle, muckle hands, and sat down on
  the sma, sma arms;
And aye she sat, and aye she reeled, and aye she wished
  for company.

In cam a sma, sma neck, and sat down on the braid, braid
  shouthers;
And aye she sat, and aye she reeled, and aye she wished
  for company.

In cam a great big head, and sat down on the sma, sma
  neck.

'What way hae ye sic braid, braid feet?' quo the wife.
'Muckle ganging, muckle ganging.'
'What way hae ye sic sma, sma legs?'
'*Aih-h-h!* – late – and *wee-e-e* – moul.'
'What way hae ye sic muckle, muckle knees?'
'Muckle praying, muckle praying.'
'What way hae ye sic sma, sma thees?'
'*Aih-h-h!* – late – and *wee-e-e* – moul.'
'What way hae ye sic big, big hips?'
'Muckle sitting, muckle sitting.'
'What way hae ye sic a sma, sma waist?'
'*Aih-h-h!* – late – and *wee-e-e* – moul.'
'What way hae ye sic braid, braid shouthers?'
'Wi carrying broom, wi carrying broom.'

> *muckle ganging*: much walking
> *late and moul*: made of dust and ashes (from the grave)

'What way hae ye sic sma, sma arms?'
'*Aih-h-h!* – late – and *wee-e-e* – moul.'
'What way hae ye sic muckle, muckle hands?'
'Threshing wi an iron flail, threshing wi an iron flail.'
'What way hae ye six a sma, sma neck?'
'*Aih-h-h!* – late – and *wee-e-e* – moul.'
'What way hae ye sic a muckle, muckle head?'
'Muckle wit, muckle wit.'
'What do ye come for?'
'For YOU!'

ANONYMOUS, SCOTTISH

COLONEL FAZACKERLEY

Colonel Fazackerley Butterworth-Toast
Bought an old castle complete with a ghost,
But someone or other forgot to declare
To Colonel Fazack that the spectre was there.

On the very first evening, while waiting to dine,
The Colonel was taking a fine sherry wine,
When the ghost, with a furious flash and a flare,
Shout out of the chimney and shivered, 'Beware!'

Colonel Fazackerley put down his glass
And said, 'My dear fellow, that's really first class!
I just can't conceive how you do it at all.
I imagine you're going to a Fancy Dress Ball?'

At this, the dread ghost gave a withering cry.
Said the Colonel (his monocle firm in his eye),
'Now just how you do it I wish I could think.
Do sit down and tell me, and please have a drink.'

The ghost in his phosphorous cloak gave a roar
And floated about between ceiling and floor.
He walked through a wall and returned through a pane
And backed up the chimney and came down again.

Said the Colonel, 'With laughter I'm feeling quite weak!'
(As trickles of merriment ran down his cheek).
'My house-warming party I hope you won't spurn.
You *must* say you'll come and you'll give us a turn!'

At this, the poor spectre – quite out of his wits –
Proceeded to shake himself almost to bits.
He rattled his chains and he clattered his bones
And he filled the whole castle with mumbles and moans.

But Colonel Fazackerley, just as before,
Was simply delighted and called out, 'Encore!'
At which the ghost vanished, his efforts in vain,
And never was seen at the castle again.

'Oh dear, what a pity!' said Colonel Fazack.
'I don't know his name, so I can't call him back.'
And then with a smile that was hard to define,
Colonel Fazackerley went in to dine.

CHARLES CAUSLEY

A BOY'S FRIEND

I have a secret friend
With whom I never quarrel.
I'm Watson to his Holmes,
He's Hardy to my Laurel.

I'm greedy for his calls
And leave him with sad heart.
He thinks of marvellous games.
He mends what comes apart.

Though when he isn't here
I can't recall his face,
I'm always glancing at
That slightly freckled space.

His name's quite ordinary
But seems unusual.
His brain's stocked like a shop.
His talk is comical.

Often with other friends
Play ends in biffs and screams:
With him, play calmly goes
Through dusk – and even dreams.

ROY FULLER

THE SECRET BROTHER

Jack lived in the green-house
When I was six,
With glass and with tomato plants,
Not with slates and bricks.

I didn't have a brother,
Jack became mine.
Nobody could see him,
He never gave a sign.

Just beyond the rockery,
By the apple-tree,
Jack and his old mother lived,
Only for me.

With a tin telephone
Held beneath the sheet,
I would talk to Jack each night.
We would never meet.

Once my sister caught me,
Said, 'He isn't there.
Down among the flower-pots
Cramm the gardener

Is the only person.'
I said nothing, but
Let her go on talking.
Yet I moved Jack out.

He and his old mother
Did a midnight flit.
No one knew his number:
I had altered it.

Only I could see
The sagging washing-line
And my brother making
Our own secret sign.

ELIZABETH JENNINGS

DICKY

Mother Oh, what a heavy sigh!
      Dicky, are you ailing?

Dicky Even by the fireside, Mother,
      My heart is failing.

  Tonight across the down,
      Whistling and jolly,
  I sauntered out from town
      With my stick of holly.

  Bounteous and cool from sea
      The wind was blowing,
  Cloud shadows under the moon
      Coming and going.

I sang old country songs,
    Ran and leaped quick,
And turned home by St Swithin's
    Twirling my stick.

And there, as I was passing
    The churchyard gate,
An old man stopped me: 'Dicky,
    You're walking late.'

I did not know the man,
    I grew afeared
At his lean, lolling jaw,
    His spreading beard.

His garments old and musty,
    Of antique cut,
His body very frail and bony,
    His eyes tight shut.

Oh, even to tell it now
    My courage ebbs . . .
His face was clay, Mother,
    His beard, cobwebs.

In that long horrid pause
    'Good night,' he said,
Entered and clicked the gate:
    'Each to his bed.'

Mother   Do not sigh or fear, Dicky;
    How is it right
To grudge the dead their ghostly dark
    And wan moonlight?

We have the glorious sun,
   Lamp and fireside.
Grudge not the dead their moonbeams
   When abroad they ride.

ROBERT GRAVES

THE KNIGHT'S GHOST

'There is a fashion in this land,
   And even come to this country,
That every lady should meet her lord
   When he is newly come frae sea:

'Some wi hawks, and some wi hounds,
   And other some wi gay monie;
But I will gae myself alone,
   And set his young son on his knee.'

She's taen her young son in her arms,
   And nimbly walkd by yon sea-strand,
And there she spy'd her father's ship,
   As she was sailing to dry land.

'Where hae ye put my ain gude lord,
   This day he stays sae far frae me?'
'If ye be wanting your ain gude lord,
   A sight o him ye'll never see.'

'Was he brunt? or was he shot?
   Or was he drowned in the sea?
Or what's become o my ain gude lord,
   That he will neer appear to me?'

'He wasna brunt, nor was he shot,
　　Nor was he drowned in the sea;
He was slain in Dumfermling
　　A fatal day to you and me.'

'Come in, come in, my merry young men,
　　Come in and drink the wine wi me;
And a' the better ye shall fare
　　For this gude news ye tell to me.'

She's brought them down to yon cellar,
　　She brought them fifty steps and three;
She birled wi them the beer and wine,
　　Till they were as drunk as drunk could be.

Then she has lockd her cellar-door,
　　For there were fifty steps and three:
'Lie there, wi my sad malison,
　　For this bad news ye've tauld to me.'

She's taen the keys intill her hand
　　And threw them deep, deep in the sea:
'Lie there, wi my sad malison,
　　Till my gude lord return to me.'

Then she sat down in her own room,
　　And sorrow lulld her fast asleep,
And up it starts her own gude lord,
　　And even at that lady's feet.

　　　　　brunt : burnt
　　　　　birled : given plenty of drink
　　　　　malison : curse

'Take here the keys, Janet,' he says,
  'That ye threw deep, deep in the sea;
And ye'll relieve my merry young men,
  For they've nane o the swick o me.

'They shot the shot, and drew the stroke,
  And wad in red bluid to the knee;
Nae sailors mair for their lord coud do
  Nor my young men they did for me.'

'I hae a question at you to ask,
  Before that ye depart frae me;
You'll tell to me what day I'll die,
  And what day will my burial be?'

'I hae nae mair o God's power
  Than he has granted unto me;
But come to heaven when ye will,
  There porter to you I will be.

'But ye'll be wed to a finer knight
  Than ever was in my degree;
Unto him ye'll hae children nine,
  And six o them will be ladies free.

'The other three will be bold young men,
  To fight for king and countrie;
The ane a duke, the second a knight,
  And third a laird o lands sae free.'

ANONYMOUS

swick : blame   *wad :* waded

LORD COZENS HARDY

Oh Lord Cozens Hardy
 Your mausoleum is cold,
The dry brown grass is brittle
 And frozen hard the mould
And where those Grecian columns rise
 So white among the dark
Of yew trees and of hollies in
 That corner of the park
By Norfolk oaks surrounded
 Whose branches seem to talk,
I know, Lord Cozens Hardy,
 I would not like to walk.

And even in the summer,
 On a bright East-Anglian day
When round your Doric portico
 Your children's children play
There's a something in the stillness
 And our waiting eyes are drawn
From the butler and the footman
 Bringing tea out on the lawn,
From the little silver spirit lamp
 That burns so blue and still,
To the half-seen mausoleum
 In the oak trees on the hill.

But when, Lord Cozens Hardy,
 November stars are bright,
And the King's Head Inn at Letheringsett
 Is shutting for the night,

mausoleum : a building that is both a tomb and a monument

The villagers have told me
　That they do not like to pass
Near your curious mausoleum
　Moon-shadowed on the grass
For fear of seeing walking
　In the season of All Souls
That first Lord Cozens Hardy,
　The Master of the Rolls.

JOHN BETJEMAN

THE YOUTH WITH THE RED-GOLD
HAIR

The gold-armoured ghost from the Roman road
Sighed over the wheat
'Fear not the sound and the glamour
Of my gold armour –
(The sound of the wind and the wheat)
Fear not its clamour . . .
Fear only the red-gold sun with the fleece of a fox
Who will steal the fluttering bird you hide in your breast.
Fear only the red-gold rain
That will dim your brightness, O my tall tower of the
　corn,
You, – my blonde girl . . .'
But the wind sighed 'Rest' . . .
The wind in his grey knight's armour –
The wind in his grey night armour –
Sighed over the fields of the wheat, 'He is gone . . .
　Forlorn.'

EDITH SITWELL

115

SHADWELL STAIR

I am the ghost of Shadwell Stair.
 Along the wharves by the water-house,
 And through the dripping slaughter-house,
I am the shadow that walks there.

Yet I have flesh both firm and cool,
 And eyes tumultuous as the gems
 Of moons and lamps in the lapping Thames
When dusk sails wavering down the pool.

Shuddering the purple street-arc burns
 Where I watch always; from the banks
 Dolorously the shipping clanks,
And after me a strange tide turns.

I walk till the stars of London wane
 And dawn creeps up the Shadwell Stair.
 But when the crowing syrens blare
I with another ghost am lain.

WILFRED OWEN

CITY

When the great bell
BOOMS over the Portland stone urn, and
From the carved cedar wood
Rises the odour of incense,
I SIT DOWN
In St Botolph Bishopsgate Churchyard
And wait for the spirit of my grandfather
Toddling along from the Barbican.

JOHN BETJEMAN

SALLY SIMPKIN'S LAMENT;

OR

JOHN JONES'S KIT-CAT-ASTROPHE

'Oh! what is that comes gliding in,
    And quite in middling haste?
It is the picture of my Jones,
    And painted to the waist.

'It is not painted to the life,
    For where's the trousers blue?
Oh, Jones, my dear! – Oh, dear! my Jones,
    What is become of you?'

'Oh Sally, dear, it is too true,
    The half that you remark
Is come to say my other half
    Is bit off by a shark!

'Oh! Sally, sharks do things by halves,
    Yet most completely do!
A bite in one place seems enough,
    But I've been bit in two.

'You know I once was all your own,
    But now a shark must share!
But let that pass – for now to you
    I'm neither here nor there.

'Alas! Death has a strange divorce
    Effected in the sea,
It has divided me from you,
    And even me from me.

'Don't fear my ghost will walk o' nights
    To haunt, as people say;
My ghost *can't* walk, for, oh! my legs
    Are many leagues away!

'Lord! think when I am swimming round
    And looking where the boat is,
A shark just snaps away a *half*
    Without "a *quarter*'s notice".

'One half is here, the other half
    Is near Columbia placed;
Oh! Sally, I have got the whole
    Atlantic for my waist.

'But now, adieu – a long adieu!
    I've solved death's awful riddle,
And would say more, but I am doomed
    To break off in the middle!'

THOMAS HOOD

THE SPUNKY

The Spunky he went like a sad little flame,
All, all alone.
All out on the zogs and a-down the lane,
All, all alone.
A tinker came by that was full of ale,
And into the mud he went head over tail,
All, all alone.

A crotchety Farmer came riding by,
All, all alone.
He cursed him low and he cursed him high,
All, all alone.
The Spunky he up and he led him astray,
The pony were foundered until it were day,
All, all alone.

There came an old Granny – she see the small Ghost,
All, all alone.
'Yew poor liddle soul all a-cold, a-lost,
All, all alone.
I'll give 'ee a criss-cross to save 'ee bide;
Be off to the Church and make merry inside,
All, all alone.'

The Spunky he laughed, 'Here I'll galley no more!'
All, all alone.
And off he did wiver and in at the door,
All, all alone.
The souls they did sing for to end his pain,
There's no little Spunky a-down the lane,
All, all alone.

ANONYMOUS

A spunky is a Will o' the wisp, Jack o' the lantern, or Fair Maid of Ireland,
believed to be the wandering spirit of a stillborn baby, or else of one who
has died before being christened. It was thought to beckon passers-by
towards the 'zogs', or marshes, because it wished to be baptized with a
'criss-cross'. To 'galley' means to frighten and to 'wiver' is to waver and
quiver.

THE GLIMPSE

She sped through the door
And, following in haste,
And stirred to the core,
I entered hot-faced;
But I could not find her,
No sign was behind her.
'Where is she?' I said:
– 'Who?' they asked that sat there;
'Not a soul's come in sight.'
– 'A maid with red hair.'
– 'Ah.' They paled. 'She is dead.
People see her at night,
But you are the first
On whom she has burst
In the keen common light.'

It was ages ago,
When I was quite strong:
I have waited since, – O,
I have waited so long!
– Yea, I set me to own
The house, where now lone
I dwell in void rooms
Booming hollow as tombs!
But I never come near her,
Though nightly, I hear her.
And my cheek has grown thin
And my hair has grown gray
With this waiting therein;
But she still keeps away!

THOMAS HARDY

THE GHOST

Opening up the house
After three weeks away
I found bird droppings
All over the ground floor,
White and heavy on the windows,
On the worktop,
On the cupboards,
On every wild hope of freedom.

I could not find any bird
At first, and feared
Some science fiction mystery,
To be horribly explained,
As soon as whatever
It was felt sure
It had got me alone,
A mile from the village.

At last I discovered him,
Weightless and out of the running,
More null than old wrapping paper
A month after Christmas.
No food inside him, of course,
He had died of hunger
And no waste either,
He was quite empty.

His desperate ghost
Flew down my throat and my ears.
There was no air
He had not suffered in.
He lay in one place,
His droppings were everywhere,
More vivid, more terrible
Than he had been, ever.

PATRICIA BEER

THE BALLAD OF KEITH OF RAVELSTON

The murmur of the mourning ghost
   That keeps the shadowy kine,
'O Keith of Ravelston,
   The sorrows of thy line!'

Ravelston, Ravelston,
   The merry path that leads
Down the golden morning hill,
   And thro' the silver meads;

Ravelston, Ravelston,
   The stile beneath the tree,
The maid that kept her mother's kine,
   The song that sang she!

She sang her song, she kept her kine,
   She sat beneath the thorn,
When Andrew Keith of Ravelston
   Rode thro' the Monday morn.

His henchmen sing, his hawk-bells ring,
  His belted jewels shine;
O Keith of Ravelston,
  The sorrows of thy line!

Year after year, where Andrew came,
  Comes evening down the glade,
And still there sits a moonshine ghost
  Where sat the sunshine maid.

Her misty hair is faint and fair,
  She keeps the shadowy kine;
O Keith of Ravelston,
  The sorrows of thy line!

I lay my hand upon the stile,
  The stile is lone and cold,
The burnie that goes babbling by
  Says naught that can be told.

Yet, stranger! here, from year to year,
  She keeps her shadowy kine;
O Keith of Ravelston,
  The sorrows of thy line!

Step out three steps, where Andrew stood –
  Why blanch thy cheeks for fear?
The ancient stile is not alone,
  'Tis not the burn I hear!

She makes her immemorial moan,
  She keeps her shadowy kine;
O Keith of Ravelston,
  The sorrows of thy line!

SYDNEY DOBELL

AT HOME

When I was dead, my spirit turned
   To seek the much-frequented house:
I passed the door, and saw my friends
   Feasting beneath the green orange boughs;
From hand to hand they pushed the wine,
   They sucked the pulp of plum and peach;
They sang, they jested, and they laughed,
   For each was loved of each.

I listened to their honest chat:
   Said one: 'To-morrow we shall be
Plod plod along the featureless sands
   And coasting miles and miles of sea.'
Said one: 'Before the turn of tide
   We will achieve the eyrie-seat.'
Said one: 'To-morrow shall be like
   To-day, but much more sweet.'

'To-morrow,' said they, strong with hope,
   And dwelt upon the pleasant way:
'To-morrow,' cried they one and all,
   While no one spoke of yesterday.
Their life stood full at blessed noon;
   I, only I, had passed away:
'To-morrow and to-day,' they cried;
   I was of yesterday.

I shivered comfortless, but cast
   No chill across the tablecloth;
I all-forgotten shivered, sad
   To stay and yet to part how loth:

I passed from the familiar room,
   I who from love had passed away,
Like the remembrance of a guest
   That tarrieth but a day.

CHRISTINA ROSSETTI

SWEET WILLIAM'S GHOST

There came a ghost to Margret's door,
   With many a grievous groan,
And ay he tirled at the pin;
   But answer made she none.

Is this my father Philip?
   Or is't my brother John?
Or is't my true love Willie,
   From Scotland new come home?

'Tis not thy father Philip;
   Nor yet thy brother John:
But tis thy true love Willie
   From Scotland new come home.

O sweet Margret! O dear Margret!
   I pray thee speak to me:
Give me my faith and troth, Margret,
   As I gave it to thee.

Thy faith and troth thou'se never get,
   Of me shalt never win,
Till that thou come within my bower,
   And kiss my cheek and chin.

If I should come within thy bower,
    I am no earthly man:
And should I kiss thy rosy lip,
    Thy days will not be long.

O sweet Margret, O dear Margret,
    I pray thee speak to me:
Give me my faith and troth, Margret,
    As I gave it to thee.

Thy faith and troth thou'se never get,
    Of me shalt never win,
Till thou take me to yon kirk yard,
    And wed me with a ring.

My bones are buried in a kirk yard
    Afar beyond the sea,
And it is but my sprite, Margret,
    That's speaking now to thee.

She stretched out her lily-white hand,
    As for to do her best:
Hae there your faith and troth, Willie,
    God send your soul good rest.

Now she has kilted her robes of green,
    A piece below her knee:
And a' the live-long winter night
    The dead corpse followed she.

Is there any room at your head, Willie?
    Or any room at your feet?
Or any room at your side, Willie,
    Wherein that I may creep?

tirled at the pin: rattled at the door-fastening

There's nae room at my head, Margret,
  There's nae room at my feet,
There's nae room at my side, Margret,
  My coffin is made so meet.

Then up and crew the red red cock,
  And up then crew the gray:
'Tis time, 'tis time, my dear Margret,
  That I were gone away.

No more the ghost to Margret said,
  But, with a grievous groan,
Evanish'd in a cloud of mist,
  And left her all alone.

O stay, my only true love, stay,
  The constant Margret cried:
Wan grew her cheeks, she clos'd her een,
  Stretch'd her soft limbs, and died.

ANONYMOUS

evanished: vanished   *een*: eyes

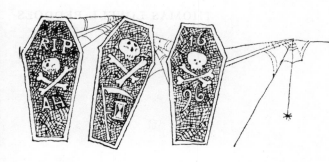

THE PHANTOM-LOVER

A ghost, that loved a lady fair,
Ever in the starry air
  Of midnight at her pillow stood;
And, with a sweetness skies above
The luring words of human love,
  Her soul the phantom wooed.
Sweet and sweet is their poisoned note,
The little snakes of silver throat,
In mossy skulls that nest and lie,
Ever singing 'die, oh! die.'

Young soul put off your flesh, and come
With me into the quiet tomb,
  Our bed is lovely, dark, and sweet;
The earth will swing us, as she goes,
Beneath our coverlid of snows,
  And the warm leaden sheet.
Dear and dear is their poisoned note,
The little snakes of silver throat,
In mossy skulls that nest and lie,
Ever singing 'die, oh! die.'

THOMAS LOVELL BEDDOES

THE GHOSTS' HIGH NOON

When the night wind howls in the chimney cowls, and
the bat in the moonlight flies,
And inky clouds, like funeral shrouds, sail over the
midnight skies –
When the footpads quail at the night-bird's wail, and
black dogs bay the moon,
Then is the spectres' holiday – then is the ghosts' high
noon!

As the sob of the breeze sweeps over the trees, and the
mists lie low on the fen,
From grey tombstones are gathered the bones that once
were women and men,
And away they go, with a mop and a mow, to the revel
that ends too soon,
For cockcrow limits our holiday – the dead of the night's
high noon!

And then each ghost with his ladye-toast to their churchyard beds take flight,
With a kiss, perhaps, on her lantern chaps, and a grisly
grim 'good night';
Till the welcome knell of the midnight bell rings forth its
jolliest tune,
And ushers our next high holiday – the dead of the night's
high noon!

W. S. GILBERT

THE GREAT AUK'S GHOST

The Great Auk's ghost rose on one leg,
Sighed thrice and three times winkt,
And turned and poached a phantom egg,
And muttered, 'I'm extinct.'

RALPH HODGSON

THE TOTEM POLE

Though all should pass with careless look,
O book
That is my boomerang and spear,
It is my heart lies buried here.

MARY GILMORE

TWELVE MEN'S MOOR

(North Cornwall)

Who shaped me like a cromlech?
Who holed me like a crickstone?
Who rocked me like a logan?
Who enchanted me like ninemaidens?
Who blessed me like a holywell?
Who bloodied me like a tinstream?
Who lit me like a wrecker's lantern?
Who blinded me like an engine-house?
Who corroded me like an arsenic-flue?
Who deepened me like a shaft?
Who emptied me like a chapel?
Who built me and left me like scaffolding?

D. M. THOMAS

RIGHT CHEEK! LEFT CHEEK!

Right cheek! left cheek! why do you burn?
Curst be she that doth me any harm;
If she be a maid, let her be staid;
If she be a widow, long let her mourn;
But if it be my own true love – burn, cheek, burn!

ANONYMOUS

It was once thought that if your cheeks burned, someone was speaking ill of you.

ST LEVAN'S PROPHECY

When with panniers astride,
A pack-horse one can ride
Through St Levan's stone,
The world will be done.

ANONYMOUS

'On the south side of the churchyard at St Levan's (near Land's End), is a granite rock, with a narrow fissure. Here, it is said, St Levan used to rest; but one day he knocked it with his fist, and it cracked through. He then uttered over it a prophecy, familiar to every child in the neighbourhood.'

From Bygone days in Devonshire and Cornwall
by Mrs Henry Pennell Whitcombe, 1874

ENCHANTMENTS

CRICKSTONE

(*West Cornwall*)

Men an Tol
Through thee I crawl.

Holed grey stone
Knit the bone;

Holed grey boulder
Straighten the shoulder;

Adder's lintel
Make me gentle;

Hole of the rain
Charm the migraine;

Stone figure nought
Strengthen the heart;

Hole of the wind
Straighten the mind;

Nose-ring on rockbeast
Bring up harvest;

Ring of granite
Straighten the planet.

D. M. THOMAS

THE WELL OF ST KEYNE

In name, in shape, in quality,
    This well is very quaint;
The name to lot of Keyne befell,
    No over-holy saint.
The shape – four trees of divers kinds,
    Withy, oak, elm, and ash
Make with their roots an arched roof,
    Whose floor this spring doth wash.
The quality – that man or wife,
    Whose chance or choice attains,
First of this sacred stream to drink,
    Thereby the mast'ry gains.

RICHARD CAREW

The well of St Keyne, perhaps the most famous holy well in the country, is near Liskeard in Cornwall. It has often been the scene of a race between a newly wedded couple. The first one there is held to be the senior partner in the marriage.

AN OLD AND CRUMBLING PARAPET

An old and crumbling parapet
Arose out of the dancing sea –
And on its top there sat a flea
For reasons which I quite forget,
But as the sun descended, and
The moon uprose across the sky,
We were alone, the flea and I,
And so I took it by the hand

And whispered, 'On your parapet
D'you think that there'd be room for me?'
'I cannot say,' replied the flea,
'I'm studying the Alphabet.'

But that was long ago, and saints
Have died since then – and Ogres bled.
And purple tigers flopped down dead
Among the pictures and the paints.

MERVYN PEAKE

THE CHOUGH

At the London Zoo

So you've got King Arthur's soul inside you, have you?
You certainly look it, gazing
Over your aristocratic, arched, and vintage
Coral bill. Your nostrils
Are covered with soft plumes, and not with bristles
Like the crows with which you are usually classified.
Sundeval, I know, that square-headed Swede,
Put you in the phalanx *Humilinares*,
Or 'humble-nostrils', amongst a flock of starlings.
I trust you regret that. '*Ay-ow, ay-ow*' you cry
With an accent indistinguishable from
The jackdaws which replace you. You are no longer
Cornish; you are barely Welsh, or Manx.
You are in mourning for something.
For you, like others, palpably must
Become extinct, unless kept in a cage.

JOHN HEATH-STUBBS

It is a very old Cornish belief that the spirit of King Arthur lives on in the chough.

THEN QUICKLY ROSE
SIR BEDIVERE

Then quickly rose Sir Bedivere, and ran,
And, leaping down the ridges lightly, plunged
Among the bulrush beds, and clutch'd the sword,
And strongly wheel'd and threw it. The great brand
Made lightnings in the splendour of the moon,
And flashing round and round, and whirl'd in an arch,
Shot like a streamer of the northern morn,
Seen where the moving isles of winter shock
By night, with noises of the Northern Sea.
So flash'd and fell the brand Excalibur:
But ere he dipt the surface, rose an arm
Clothed in white samite, mystic, wonderful,
And caught him by the hilt, and brandish'd him
Three times, and drew him under in the mere.
And lightly went the other to the King.

ALFRED, LORD TENNYSON
From *The Passing of Arthur*

ROBIN SONG

I am the hunted king
  Of the frost and big icicles
  And the bogey cold
  With its wind boots.

I am the uncrowned
  Of the rainworld
  Hunted by lightning and thunder
  And rivers.

I am the lost child
  Of the wind
  Who goes through me looking for something else
  Who can't recognize me though I cry.

I am the maker
  Of the world
  That rolls to crush
  And silence my knowledge.

TED HUGHES

THE SCARECROW IN
THE SCHOOLMASTER'S OATS

Hail, Mister Snowman. Farewell,
Gray consumptive.

Rain. A sleeve dripping.
Broken mirrors all about me.

A thrush laid eggs in my pocket.
My April coat was one long rapture.

I push back green spume, yellow breakers.
King Canute.

One morning I handled infinite gold,
King Midas.

I do not trust Ikey the tinker.
He has a worse coat.

A Hogmanay sun the colour of whisky
Seeps through my rags.
I am – what you guess – King Barleycorn.

GEORGE MACKAY BROWN

SONG FOR THE SPINNING WHEEL

An old Westmorland belief

Swiftly turn the murmuring wheel!
Night has brought the welcome hour,
When the weary fingers feel
Help, as if from faery power;
Dewy night o'ershades the ground;
Turn the swift wheel round and round!

Now, beneath the starry sky,
Couch the widely-scattered sheep; –
Ply the pleasant labour, ply!
For the spindle, while they sleep,
Runs with speed more smooth and fine,
Gathering up a trustier line.

Short-lived likings may be bred
By a glance from fickle eyes;
But true love is like the thread
Which the kindly wool supplies,
When the flocks are all at rest,
Sleeping on the mountain's breast.

WILLIAM WORDSWORTH

HARP OF WILD AND DREAM-LIKE
STRAIN

Harp of wild and dream-like strain,
When I touch thy strings,
Why dost thou repeat again
Long-forgotten things?

Harp, in other, earlier days,
I could sing to thee;
And not one of all my lays
Vexed my memory.

But now, if I awake a note
That gave me joy before,
Sounds of sorrow from thee float,
Changing evermore.

Yet, still steeped in memory's dyes,
They come sailing on,
Darkening all my summer skies,
Shutting out my sun.

EMILY BRONTË

ENCHANTMENTS

FRUTTA DI MARE

I am a sea shell flung
Up from the ancient sea;
Now I lie here, among
Roots of a tamarisk tree;
No one listens to me.

I sing to myself all day
In a husky voice, quite low,
Things the great fishes say
And you must need to know;
All night I sing just so.

But lift me from the ground,
And hearken at my rim;
Only your sorrow's sound
Amazed, perplexed and dim,
Comes coiling to the brim;

For what the wise whales ponder
Awaking out from sleep,
The key to all your wonder,
The answers of the deep,
These to myself I keep.

GEOFFREY SCOTT

O WEARY LADY, GERALDINE

O weary lady, Geraldine,
I pray you, drink this cordial wine!
It is a wine of virtuous powers;
My mother made it of wild flowers.

And will your mother pity me,
Who am a maiden most forlorn?
Christabel answered – Woe is me!
She died the hour that I was born.
I have heard the grey-haired friar tell
How on her death-bed she did say,
That she should hear the castle-bell
Strike twelve upon my wedding-day.
O mother dear! that thou wert here!
I would, said Geraldine, she were!

But soon with altered voice, said she –
'Off, wandering mother! Peak and pine!
I have power to bid thee flee.'
Alas! what ails poor Geraldine?
Why stares she with unsettled eye?
Can she the bodiless dead espy?
And why with hollow voice cries she,
'Off, woman, off! this hour is mine –
Though thou her guardian spirit be,
Off, woman, off! 'tis given to me.'

Then Christabel knelt by the lady's side,
And raised to heaven her eyes so blue –
Alas! said she, this ghastly ride –
Dear lady! it hath wildered you!
The lady wiped her moist cold brow,
And faintly said, 'Tis over now!'

Again the wild-flower wine she drank:
Her fair large eyes 'gan glitter bright,
And from the floor whereon she sank,
The lofty lady stood upright:
She was most beautiful to see,
Like a lady of a far countrée.

SAMUEL TAYLOR COLERIDGE
From *Christabel*

ARDEVORA VEOR

At turn of tide, clear sky,
Seventh September morn,
A boy goes sculling by
Down river from Ruan Lanihorne.

The secret flats of the Fal
Reveal unnumbered birds
Mirrored in quiet waters:
A world still beyond words.

Behind a screen of elms
A deserted house is there,
Haunted by its echo –
Ardevora, Ardevora veor.

A herring-bone hedge of stone,
A lodge at the entrance gate,
An orchard of unpicked apples:
For whom, or what, does it wait?

Evidences of former love
And care on every side,
The anchorage, the quay:
No one comes now at the turning of the tide.

A planted berberis sheds
Its berries on the ground;
From the windlass and the well
No movement ever, and no sound.

The pretty panes are broken,
Blackberries ripen on the wall:
Peer in through the windows,
Whence no one looks out at all.

No one looks out any longer
Across the creek to the farm;
From candle-lit doorway to attic
No signal of joy or alarm.

Nor any motion of footfall
Beneath ceiling or rafter by day;
All laughter, all merriment over,
The ghosts have their way.

A house alone with its shadows,
The floors strewn with sharp glass,
What may have happened here
At Ardevora, Ardevora veor,
What estrangement come to pass?

Only an echo replies
Into the listening morn
As the solitary sculler
Moves silently down river
With the tide from Ruan Lanihorne.

A. L. ROWSE

The place-name Ardevora Veor is in the Cornish language, and means
Great Ardevora. (*Ardevora*: height, or raised part, by the waters.)

HOUSE FEAR

Always – I tell you this they learned –
Always at night when they returned
To the lonely house from far away
To lamps unlighted and fire gone grey,
They learned to rattle the lock and key
To give whatever might chance to be
Warning and time to be off in flight:
And preferring the out- to the in-door night,
They learned to leave the house-door wide
Until they had lit the lamp inside.

ROBERT FROST

VOICES

I heard those voices today again:
Voices of women and children, down in that hollow
Of blazing light into which swoops the tree-darkened lane
Before it mounts up into the shadow again.

I turned the bend – just as always before
There was no one at all down there in the sunlit hollow;
Only ferns in the wall, foxgloves by the hanging door
Of that blind old desolate cottage. And just as before

I noticed the leaping glitter of light
Where the stream runs under the lane; in that mine-dark
  archway
– Water and stones unseen as though in the gloom of
  night –
Like glittering fish slithers and leaps the light.

I waited long at the bend of the lane,
But heard only the murmuring water under the archway.
Yet I tell you, I've been to that place again and again,
And always, in summer weather, those voices are plain,
Down near that broken house, just where the tree-
  darkened lane
Swoops into the hollow of light before mounting to
  shadow again.

FRANCES BELLERBY

DROWNED, SIR, DROWNED MEN
THE LOT OF THEM!

Innkeeper Drowned, Sir, drowned men the lot of them!
With never a white rag from the sea
For their wives to cry on.
But our son came back. Nine days he lay,
Dumb as a fish in the bed you're sleeping;
Fish indeed for mother naked he was
In a sandpool when the coastguards found him,
Netted with weed and a cry of gulls for speech.
Can a man live; can a man live
After a day and a night in the arms of the Old one?
A changed man, and never our son came back
With a froth of lies from the deep.
But then you know the story; gutter news it was
For the press has an itch for the Child and his wild
    deeds.
Near Aeaea's Point, he said, they shipped a stranger,
Then, right lads they were with a taste for gold,
Steered for the slave-coast to mart his flesh,
A paying trip in those days.
Now here's the fool-talk!
Five miles out, he swore, in a fair wind
Uprose the corded freight, bird free and smiling,
'Then will you turn,' he said to the twitching helm,
'I shipped for Naxos, man, you're making Aeaea.'
Ah, they'd have rushed to clap him in irons below,
But mark now our lunatic boy!
Vine leaves, he said, wreathing the mast, sir.
Blue grapes on the sagging cordage.
The sea breath thick with wine, and then this stranger!

Look now, you can't describe a god –
Something about his smile, our boy said.
No wonder the whole crew went mad and tumbled
    overboard.
No wonder our poor son, the sole survivor,
Drank where you're sitting now; drank, drank, drank;
Touched by the wine god.
Then never a word till he died,
But 'Zagreus', maybe or 'Child'; he'd stare to Naxos.
Some nights down at the quay we'd find him
Fumbling a boat cord as if he'd launch there.
Oh the times I've led him back asleep but struggling
Out of his father's arms to the wicked sea.
There was never an hour of peace till he died
Although we loved him.
Shock, they said, the shock of a summer storm!

THOMAS BLACKBURN
From *The Voyage Out*

The traveller spoken of in this speech is Dionysus, the Greek god who
dies and lives again, the inspirer of poets and musicians, and the god of
wine (known to the Romans as Bacchus). He married Ariadne after she
had been deserted by Theseus in Naxos. The Innkeeper in the play is
talking to Dionysus, but does not know it yet.

RHYME FOR CHILDREN

I am the seed that slept last night;
This morning I have grown upright.

Within my dream there was a king.
Now he is gone in the wide morning.

He had a queen, also a throne.
Waking, I find myself alone.

If I could have that dream again,
The seed should grow into a queen

And she should find at her right hand
A king to rule her heart and land:

And I would be the spring which burst
Beside their love and quenched their thirst.

ELIZABETH JENNINGS

I WOULD SING SONGS

I would sing songs
If I had my tune.
A cobbler has pinched it
To make four shoon.

Two pairs of shoon
And sold every stitch.
Had I kept my music
I might have been rich.

ANONYMOUS, peasant dance song;
translated from the Polish by
Jerzy Peterkiewicz and Burns Singer

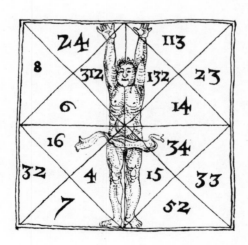

Dwarfs, Giants,
Ogres & Demons

WEE WILLIE GRAY

Wee Willie Gray, and his leather wallet,
Peel a willow-wand, to be him boots and jacket;
The rose upon the breer will be him trews and doublet,
The rose upon the breer will be him trews and doublet.

Wee Willie Gray, and his leather wallet,
Twice a lily-flower will be him sark and cravat;
Feathers of a flee wad feather up his bonnet,
Feathers of a flee wad feather up his bonnet.

ROBERT BURNS
In imitation of an old nursery song,
'Wee Totum Fogg'

trews : trousers
sark : shirt

THE WEE WEE MAN

As I was wa'king all alone,
    Between a water and a wa,
And there I spy'd a wee wee man,
    And he was the least that ere I saw.

His legs were scarce a shathmont's length,
    And thick and thimber was his thigh;
Between his brows there was a span,
    And between his shoulders there was three.

He took up a meikle stane,
    And he flang't as far as I could see;
Though I had been a Wallace wight,
    I couldna liften 't to my knee.

'O wee wee man, but thou be strang!
    O tell me where thy dwelling be?'
'My dwelling's down at yon bonny bower;
    O will you go with me and see?'

On we lap, and awa we rade,
    Till we come to yon bonny green;
We lighted down for to bait our horse,
    And out there came a lady fine.

Four and twenty at her back,
    And they were a' clad out in green;
Though the King of Scotland had been there,
    The warst o them might hae been his queen.

On we lap, and awa we rade,
　Till we came to yon bonny ha,
Whare the roof was o the beaten gould,
　And the floor was o the cristal a'.

When we came to the stair-foot,
　Ladies were dancing, jimp and sma,
But in the twinkling of an eye,
　My wee wee man was clean awa.

ANONYMOUS

shathmont : the distance from the top of the thumb to the bottom of the palm
thimber : heavy　　*meikle stane :* big stone
wight : strong　　*imp :* slim

159

ON SOME GHOSTLY COMPANIONS
AT A SPA

That was an evil day when I
To Strathpeffer drew anigh,
For there I found no human soul
But Ogres occupied the whole.

They had at first a human air
In coats and flannel underwear.
They rose and walked upon their feet
And filled their bellies full of meat.
They wiped their lips when they had done,
But they were Ogres every one.

Each issuing from his secret bower,
I marked them in the morning hour.
By limp and totter, lisp and droop,
I singled each one from the group.
I knew them all as they went by –
I knew them by their blasted eye!

Detested Ogres, from my sight
Depart to your congenial night!
From these fair vales, from this fair day,
Fleet, spectres, on your downward way,
Like changing figures in a dream,
To Muttonhole or Pittenweem!
As, by some harmony divine
The devils quartered in the swine,
If any baser place exist
In God's great registration list –
Some den with wallow and a trough –
Find it, ye ogres, and be off!

ROBERT LOUIS STEVENSON

IN THE ORCHARD

There was a giant by the Orchard Wall
Peeping about on this side and on that,
And feeling in the trees. He was as tall
As the big apple tree, and twice as fat:
His beard poked out, all bristly-black, and there
Were leaves and gorse and heather in his hair.

He held a blackthorn club in his right hand,
And plunged the other into every tree,
Searching for something – You could stand
Beside him and not reach up to his knee,
So big he was – I trembled lest he should
Come trampling, round-eyed, down to where I stood.

I tried to get away. – But, as I slid
Under a bush, he saw me, and he bent
Down deep at me, and said, '*Where is she hid?*'
I pointed over there, and off he went –

But, while he searched, I turned and simply flew
Round by the lilac bushes back to you.

JAMES STEPHENS

SONG OF THE OGRES

Little fellow, you're amusing,
Stop before you end by losing
 Your shirt:
Run along to Mother, Gus,
Those who interfere with us
 Get hurt.

Honest Virtue, old wives prattle,
Always wins the final battle.
 Dear, Dear!
Life's exactly what it looks,
Love may triumph in the books,
 Not here.

We're not joking, we assure you:
Those who rode this way before you
 Died hard.
What? Still spoiling for a fight?
Well, you've asked for it all right:
 On guard!

Always hopeful, aren't you? Don't be.
Night is falling and it won't be
 Long now:
You will never see the dawn,
You will wish you'd not been born.
 And how!

W. H. AUDEN

COLD LIES THE DEW

There was an old Granny who lost her sight,
Cold lies the Dew.
She couldn't tell if it were morning or night,
Cold lies the Dew.
There come a fine gentleman, black as a coal,
'I'll give 'ee some eyes, if you'll sell me your soul,'
Cold lies the Dew.

Singing
Green, green, green, all a-green, all a-green,
A-dancing round the Tree.

She gave him a criss-cross, she muttered a prayer,
Cold lies the Dew,
And off with a scritch he went up in the air,
Cold lies the Dew.
The poor old Granny she longed for her eyes,
And down on her knees goes her head and she cries,
Cold lies the Dew.

There came a pit-patter and Somebody says,
Cold lies the Dew.
'All you long life you've a-minded our ways,
Cold lies the Dew.
With pail of spring water and cream bowl too' –
The led her away in the May morning dew,
Cold lies the Dew.

Her sight came back, it was clear and fine,
Cold lies the Dew.
Her pretty blue eyes they was all a-shine,
Cold lies the Dew.
She stood all alone there – Then who were 'They'?
The wise old Granny she never would say,
Cold lies the Dew.

ANONYMOUS

'The Tree' is the hawthorn, which was thought to have magic properties.
The Romans put the leaves in the cradles of newly born babies as a charm
against evil spells. At one time a hawthorn on a green hillock was believed
to mark the entrance to the 'other' world.

THE DEIL'S AWA WI' TH' EXCISEMAN

Tune – *The Looking glass* or *The Hemp Dresser*

The deil cam fiddlin thro' the town,
And danc'd awa wi' th' Exciseman;
And ilka wife cries, 'Auld Mahoun,
I wish you luck o' the prize, man.'

Chorus The deil's awa, the deil's awa,
The deil's awa wi' th' Exciseman,
He's danc'd awa, he's danc'd awa,
He's danc'd awa wi' th' Exciseman.

deil : devil   *ilka :* every
Auld Mahoun : Satan, the devil

164

We'll mak our maut and we'll brew our drink,
   We'll laugh, sing, and rejoice, man!
And mony braw thanks to the meikle black deil
   That danc'd awa wi' th' Exciseman.

There's threesome reels, there's foursome reels,
   There's hornpipes and strathspeys, man,
But the ae best dance e'er cam to the Land
   Was, 'The deil's awa wi' th' Exciseman.'

ROBERT BURNS

maut : malt   *meikle:* big

Robert Burns was himself an exciseman for a time, and is said to have
written this poem by the seashore while with his fellow excisemen and
watching a suspicious brig, believed to be a smugglers' craft, sailing in
the Solway Firth in 1792.

THE START OF A MEMORABLE
HOLIDAY

Good evening, sir. Good evening, ma'am. Good evening,
   little ladies.
From all the staff, a hearty welcome to the Hotel Hades.
Oh yes, sir, since you booked your rooms we have been
   taken over
And changed our name – but for the better – as you'll
   soon discover.
Porter, Room 99! Don't worry, sir – just now he took
Much bulkier things than bags on his pathetic iron hook.

The other room, the children's room? I'm very pleased to say
We've put them in the annexe, half a mile across the way.
They'll have a nearer view there of the bats' intriguing flying,
And you, dear sir and madam, won't be troubled by their crying
– Although I'm sure that neither of them's frightened of the gloom.
Besides, the maid will try to find a candle for their room.

Of course, ma'am, we've a maid there, she's the porter's (seventh) wife:
She'll care for these dear children quite as well as her own life.
The journey's tired them? Ah, tonight they won't be counting sheep!
I'll see they have a nice hot drink before they're put to sleep.
Don't be too late yourselves, sir, for the hotel's evening meal:
I hope that on the menu will be some roast milk-fed veal.
If you'll forgive me, I must stoke the ovens right away:
It's going to be (excuse the joke) hell in this place today!
Yes, I do all the cooking *and* the getting of the meat:
Though we're so far from shops we've usually something fresh to eat.
Of course, it isn't always veal, and when the school terms start
Joints may get tougher. But our gravy still stays full of heart!

ROY FULLER

EVENTS
STRANGE
& FAMILIAR

THE THREE SINGING BIRDS

The King walked in his garden green,
  Where grew a marvellous tree;
And out of its leaves came singing birds
  By one, and two, and three.

The first bird had wings of white,
  The second had wings of gold,
The third had wings of deepest blue
  Most beauteous to behold.

The white bird flew to the northern land,
  The gold bird flew to the west,
The blue bird flew to the cold, cold south
  Where never bird might nest.

The King waited a twelvemonth long,
  Till back the three birds flew,
They lighted down upon the tree,
  The white, the gold, and the blue.

The white bird brought a pearly seed
  And gave it to the King;
The gold bird from out of the west
  He brought a golden ring.

The third bird with feathers blue
  Who came from the far cold south,
A twisted sea-shell smooth and grey
  He carried in his mouth.

The King planted the pearly seed
  Down in his garden green,
And up there sprang a pearl-white maid,
  The fairest ever seen.

She looked at the King and knelt her down
    All under the magic tree,
She smiled at him with her red lips
    But not a word said she.

Instead she took the grey sea-shell
    And held it to his ear,
She pressed it close and soon the King
    A strange, sweet song did hear.

He raised the fair maid by the hand
    Until she stood at his side;
Then he gave her the golden ring
    And took her for his bride.

And at their window sang the birds,
    They sang the whole night through,
Then off they went at break of day,
    The white, the gold, and the blue.

JAMES REEVES

CUCKOO SONG

*Spring begins in southern England on 14 April, on which
date the Old Woman lets the Cuckoo out of her basket at
Heathfield Fair – locally known as Heffle Cuckoo Fair.*

Tell it to the locked-up trees,
Cuckoo, bring your song here!
Warrant, Act and Summons, please,
For Spring to pass along here!
Tell old Winter, if he doubt,
Tell him squat and square-a!

Old Woman!
Old Woman!
Old Woman's let the Cuckoo out
At Heffle Cuckoo Fair-a!

March has searched and April tried –
'Tisn't long to May now,
Not so far to Whitsuntide
And Cuckoo's come to stay now!
Hear the valiant fellow shout
Down the orchard bare-a!
Old Woman!
Old Woman!
Old Woman's let the Cuckoo out
At Heffle Cuckoo Fair-a!

When your heart is young and gay
And the season rules it –
Work your works and play your play
'Fore the Autumn cools it!
Kiss you turn and turn-about,
But my lad, beware-a!
Old Woman!
Old Woman!
Old Woman's let the Cuckoo out
At Heffle Cuckoo Fair-a!

RUDYARD KIPLING

A RARE AND MIRACULOUS CASE

You gentlemen lend me your ears
And do not be amazed,
And all you timid women,
Do not take fright at this:
It came to pass in Ireland,
As is true beyond a question,
That there was a poor woman
Who went to ask for alms,
She had many children with her,
They were beautiful to see;
She came to beg for money,
To provide them all with food,
From Doña Margarita,
A princess, as they say,
Without peer in that country.
When she saw so many children
She asked that poor soul:
    'Are all those your own children?'
And she was answered thus:
    'Yes, my lady, by one father,
Who's still living, at your service.'
    'Impossible,' she answered,
'For I am very certain
That they're children of many fathers
As you cannot deny.'
The poor soul was afflicted
At being slandered so,
She raised her hands to heaven
And kneeled down on the ground,
And she said: 'Oh may it please God,

Who can do it if He will,
To send you so many children,
My lady, by one father,
That you won't know one from the others,
Nor be able to bring them up!'
This prayer was so acceptable
That that lady brought to birth
Three hundred and sixty children;
It was indeed a marvel!
They were all born in a single day
In pain, but with no danger,
Like little mice, they were so small,
And alive without exception.
And in a font of silver,
And by a bishop, they
Were every single one baptized,
And afterwards they went to taste
That glory which has no compare
Beyond all estimation.
That very font unto this day
In a church has been preserved,
And it was put upon display
To Charles our emperor.
And authors of great merit
To the truth of this will swear,
One is Baptista Fulgoso,
And Enrico, with Algozar,
And Doctor Vives of Valencia,
Who is not to be ignored.

Traditional Spanish;
translated by W. S. Merwin

THE SEVEN SISTERS
or, THE SOLITUDE OF BINNORIE

Seven Daughters had Lord Archibald,
All children of one mother:
You could not say in one short day
What love they bore each other.
A garland, of seven lilies wrought!
Seven Sisters that together dwell;
But he, bold Knight as ever fought,
Their Father, took of them no thought,
He loved the wars so well.
Sing, mournfully, oh! mournfully,
The solitude of Binnorie!

Fresh blows the wind, a western wind,
And from the shores of Erin,
Across the wave, a Rover brave
To Binnorie is steering:
Right onward to the Scottish strand
The gallant ship is borne;
The warriors leap upon the land,
And hark! the Leader of the band
Hath blown his bugle horn.
Sing, mournfully, oh! mournfully,
The solitude of Binnorie.

Beside a grotto of their own,
With boughs above them closing,
The Seven are laid, and in the shade
They lie like fawns reposing.
But now, upstarting with affright
At noise of man and steed,

Away they fly to left, to right –
Of your fair household, Father-Knight,
Methinks you take small heed!
Sing, mournfully, oh! mournfully,
The solitude of Binnorie.

Away the seven fair Campbells fly,
And, over hill and hollow,
With menace proud, and insult loud,
The youthful Rovers follow.
Cried they, 'Your Father loves to roam:
Enough for him to find
The empty house when he comes home;
For us your yellow ringlets comb,
For us be fair and kind!'
Sing, mournfully, oh! mournfully,
The solitude of Binnorie.

Some close behind, some side to side,
Like clouds·in stormy weather;
They run, and cry, 'Nay, let us die,
And let us die together.'
A lake was near; the shore was steep;
There never foot had been;
They ran, and with a desperate leap
Together plunged into the deep,
Nor ever more were seen.
Sing, mournfully, oh! mournfully,
The solitude of Binnorie.

The stream that flows out of the lake,
As through the glen it rambles,
Repeats a moan o'er moss and stone,
For those seven lovely Campbells.

Seven little Islands, green and bare,
Have risen from out the deep:
The fishers say, those sisters fair
By faeries all are buried there,
And there together sleep.
Sing, mournfully, oh! mournfully,
The solitude of Binnorie.

WILLIAM WORDSWORTH

A SMALL DRAGON

I've found a small dragon in the woodshed.
Think it must have come from deep inside a forest
because it's damp and green and leaves
are still reflecting in its eyes.

I fed it on many things, tried grass,
the roots of stars, hazel–nut and dandelion,
but it stared up at me as if to say, I need
foods you can't provide.

It made a nest among the coal,
not unlike a bird's but larger,
it is out of place here
and is quite silent.

If you believed in it I would come
hurrying to your house to let you share my wonder,
but I want instead to see
if you yourself will pass this way.

BRIAN PATTEN

THE SERPENT

There was a Serpent who had to sing.
There was. There was.
He simply gave up Serpenting.
Because. Because.

He didn't like his Kind of Life;
He couldn't find a proper Wife;
He was a Serpent with a soul;
He got no Pleasure down his Hole.
And so, of course, he had to Sing,
And Sing he did, like Anything!
The Birds, they were, they were Astounded;
And various Measures Propounded
To stop the Serpent's Awful Racket:
They bought a Drum. He wouldn't Whack it.
They sent, – you always send, – to Cuba
And got a Most Commodious Tuba;
They got a Horn, they got a Flute,
But Nothing would suit.
He said, 'Look, Birds, all this is futile:
I do *not* like to Bang or Tootle.'
And then he cut loose with a Horrible Note
That practically split the Top of his Throat.
'You see,' he said, with a Serpent's Leer,
'I'm Serious about my Singing Career!'
And the Woods Resounded with many a Shriek
As the Birds flew off to the End of Next Week.

THEODORE ROETHKE

THE ROC

Scattered like flotsam on the erupting sea
   When the ship cracked, Sinbad and his sailors
      Gasped for air, clung to planks and oars,
Then struggled madly for the beach. Some three
Who managed to escape the crags were thrown
   On yellow sand, and fell asleep at once,
      Soaked through but too exhausted to take shelter,
And slept like dead men till next day at noon.

On waking, someone noticed a black cloud
   Descending over them, like a huge raven
      With curved bill, wings, extended talons,
And voice of thunder, distant but quite loud.
Sinbad grew pale, trembled and shouted, 'Quick,
   Find shelter somewhere; this is the great Roc,
      The bird of prey with wingspan of a mile!
Run to that cave; don't stop to have a look!'

They reached the grotto just in time, – the sky
   Had grown pitch-black, the wingbeats were a gale;
      But, safe in hiding, Sinbad laughed: 'A miracle!
It's not the Roc that's huge, but you and I,
My sailors, who are small, and growing smaller;
   Soon we'll be microscopic, and that crow –
      As harmless as a lion to a gnat –
Won't even notice when we choose to go.'

EDWARD LOWBURY

VISION OF BELSHAZZAR

The King was on his throne,
    The Satraps throng'd the hall:
A thousand bright lamps shone
    O'er that high festival.
A thousand cups of gold,
    In Judah deem'd divine –
Jehovah's vessels hold
    The godless Heathen's wine!

In that same hour and hall,
    The fingers of a hand
Came forth against the wall,
    And wrote as if on sand:
The fingers of a man; –
    A solitary hand
Along the letters ran,
    And traced them like a wand.

The monarch saw, and shook,
    And bade no more rejoice;
All bloodless wax'd his look,
    And tremulous his voice.
'Let the men of lore appear,
    The wisest of the earth,
And expound the words of fear,
    Which mar our royal mirth.'

Chaldea's seers are good,
    But here they have no skill;
And the unknown letters stood
    Untold and awful still.

satrap : a provincial governor in ancient Persia

179

And Babel's men of age
  Are wise and deep in lore;
But now they were not sage,
  They saw – but knew no more.

A captive in the land,
  A stranger and a youth,
He heard the king's command,
  He saw that writing's truth.
The lamps around were bright.
  The prophecy in view;
He read it on that night, –
  The morrow proved it true.

'Belshazzar's grave is made,
  His kingdom pass'd away,
He, in the balance weigh'd,
  Is light and worthless clay;
The shroud his robe of state,
  His canopy the stone;
The Mede is at his gate!
  The Persian on his throne!'

GEORGE GORDON, LORD BYRON
(See the Old Testament Book of Daniel, Chapter 5)

THE CAP AND BELLS

The jester walked in the garden:
The garden had fallen still;
He bade his soul rise upward
And stand on her window-sill.

It rose in a straight blue garment,
When owls began to call:
It had grown wise-tongued by thinking
Of a quiet and light footfall;

But the young queen would not listen;
She rose in her pale night-gown;
She drew in the heavy casement
And pushed the latches down.

He bade his heart go to her,
When the owls called out no more;
In a red and quivering garment
It sang to her through the door.

It had grown sweet-tongued by dreaming
Of a flutter of flower-like hair;
But she took up her fan from the table
And waved it off on the air.

'I have cap and bells,' he pondered,
'I will send them to her and die';
And when the morning whitened
He left them where she went by.

She laid them upon her bosom,
Under a cloud of her hair,
And her red lips sang them a love-song
Till stars grew out of the air.

She opened her door and her window,
And the heart and the soul came through,
To her right hand came the red one,
To her left hand came the blue.

They set up a noise like crickets,
A chattering wise and sweet,
And her hair was a folded flower
And the quiet of love in her feet.

W. B. YEATS

UP ON THE DOWNS

Up on the downs the red-eyed kestrels hover,
Eyeing the grass.
The field-mouse flits like a shadow into cover
As their shadows pass.

Men are burning the gorse on the down's shoulder;
A drift of smoke
Glitters with fire and hangs, and the skies smoulder,
And the lungs choke.

Once the tribe did thus on the downs, on these downs
     burning
Men in the frame.
Crying to the gods of the downs till their brains were
     turning
And the gods came.

And to-day on the downs, in the wind, the hawks, the
     grasses,
In blood and air,
Something passes me and cries as it passes.
On the chalk downland bare.

JOHN MASEFIELD

SILENT IS THE HOUSE – ALL ARE LAID ASLEEP

Silent is the House – all are laid asleep;
One, alone, looks out o'er the snow wreaths deep;
Watching every cloud, dreading every breeze
That whirls the 'wildering drifts and bends the groaning
    trees.

Cheerful is the hearth, soft the matted floor;
Not one shivering gust creeps through pane or door;
The little lamp burns straight, its rays shoot strong and
    far;
I trim it well to be the Wanderer's guiding-star.

Frown, my haughty sire; chide, my angry dame;
Set your slaves to spy, threaten me with shame:
But neither sire nor dame, nor prying serf shall know
What angel nightly tracks that waste of winter snow.

What I love shall come like visitant of air,
Save in secret power from lurking human snare;
Who loves me, no word of mine shall e'er betray,
Though for faith unstained my life must forfeit pay.

Burn, then, little lamp; glimmer straight and clear –
Hush! a rustling wing stirs, methinks, the air:
He for whom I wait, thus ever comes to me;
Strange Power! I trust thy might; trust thou my
    constancy.

EMILY BRONTË

ENDS MEET

My grandmother came down the steps into the garden.
She shone in the gauzy air.
She said: 'There's an old woman at the gate –
See what she wants, my dear.'

My grandmother's eyes were blue like the damsels
Darting and swerving above the stream,
Or like the kingfisher arrow shot into darkness
Through the archway's dripping gleam.

My grandmother's hair was silver as sunlight.
The sun had been poured right over her, I saw,
And ran down her dress and spread a pool for her
    shadow
To float in. And she would live for evermore.

There was nobody at the gate when I got there.
Not even a shadow hauling along the road,
Nor my yellow snail delicate under the ivy,
Nor my sheltering cold-stone toad.

But the sunflowers aloft were calm. They'd seen no one.
They were sucking light, for ever and a day.
So I busied myself with going away unheeded
And with having nothing to say.

No comment, nothing to tell, or to think,
Whilst the day followed the homing sun.
There was no old woman at my grandmother's gate.

And there isn't at mine.

FRANCES BELLERBY

damsels: damsel-flies, a smaller, sub-order of dragonflies

I SAW A STRANGE CREATURE

I saw a strange creature,
a bright ship of the air beautifully adorned,
bearing away plunder between her horns,
fetching it home from a foray.
She was minded to build a bower in her stronghold,
and construct it with cunning if she could do so.
But then a mighty creature appeared over the mountain
whose face is familiar to all dwellers on earth;
he seized on his treasure and sent home the wanderer
much against her will; she went westward
harbouring hostility, hastening forth.
Dust lifted to heaven; dew fell on the earth,
night fled hence; and no man knew
thereafter, where that strange creature went.

ANGLO-SAXON RIDDLE;
translated by Kevin Crossley-Holland

Answer: sun and moon

SONG

A sunny shaft did I behold,
  From sky to earth it slanted:
And poised therein a bird so bold –
  Sweet bird, thou wert enchanted!

He sank, he rose, he twinkled, he trolled
  Within that shaft of sunny mist;
His eyes of fire, his beak of gold,
  All else of amethyst!

And thus he sang: 'Adieu! adieu!
Love's dreams prove seldom true.
The blossoms they make no delay:
The sparkling dew-drops will not stay.
  Sweet month of May,
    We must away;
      Far, far away!
      Today! today!'

SAMUEL TAYLOR COLERIDGE
From *Zapolya*

WINDY NIGHTS

Whenever the moon and stars are set,
   Whenever the wind is high,
All night long in the dark and wet,
   A man goes riding by.
Late in the night when the fires are out,
Why does he gallop and gallop about?

Whenever the trees are crying aloud,
   And ships are tossed at sea,
By, on the highway, low and loud,
   By at the gallop goes he.
By at the gallop he goes, and then
By he comes back at the gallop again.

ROBERT LOUIS STEVENSON

KINGDOM OF MIST

I ride through a kingdom of mist
where farms drown in a phantom sea
and May piles up in the hedge like snow
waiting to melt in tomorrow's sun.

Young wheat lies down where May-winds blew
and larks are earthbound by the stars.
A heron glides between the trees
that hold the river to its course.

Here pebbles slowly turn to snails
and spiders' webs are spun with glass.
Small shells fly off as frightened moths
and cows become as druid stones.

Only the mist moves as a ghost
loving the land with limbs of fur
and whispered words grow grey as breath
rising into the frosting air.

And night comes down where day once grew,
lights ripple through this thin white sea,
while in the village children sleep
never to know they slept in sky.

EDWARD STOREY

STONES

On the flat of the earth lie
Stones, their eyes turned
To the earth's centre, always.
If you throw them they fly
Grudgingly, measuring your arm's
Weak curve before homing
To a place they know.

Digging, we may jostle
Stones with our thin tines
Into stumbling activity.
Small ones move most.
When we turn from them
They grumble to a still place.
It can take a month to grate

That one inch. Watch how stones
Clutter together on hills
And beaches, settling heavily
In unremarkable patterns.
A single stone can vanish
In a black night, making
Someone bury it in water.

We can polish some;
Onyx, perhaps, chalcedony,
Jasper and quartzite from
The edges of hard land.
But we do not alter them.
Once in a million years
Their stone hearts lurch.

LESLIE NORRIS

tines: prongs on a fork

TOM BONE

My name is Tom Bone,
I live all alone
In a deep house on Winter Street.
    Through my mud wall
    The wolf-spiders crawl
    And the mole has his beat.

On my roof of green grass
All the day footsteps pass
In the heat and the cold,
    As snug in a bed
    With my name at its head
    One great secret I hold.

Tom Bone, when the owls rise
In the drifting night skies
Do you walk round about?
    All the solemn hours through
    I lie down just like you
    And sleep the night out.

Tom Bone, as you lie there
On your pillow of hair,
What grave thoughts do you keep?
    Tom says, Nonsense and stuff!
    You'll know soon enough.
    Sleep, darling, sleep.

CHARLES CAUSLEY

CHECK

The Night was creeping on the ground!
She crept, and did not make a sound

Until she reached the tree: And then
She covered it, and stole again

Along the grass beside the wall!
– I heard the rustling of her shawl

As she threw blackness everywhere
Along the sky, the ground, the air,

And in the room where I was hid!
But, no matter what she did

To everything that was without,
She could not put my candle out!

So I stared at the Night! And she
Stared back solemnly at me!

JAMES STEPHENS

Salt Water Spirits
Fresh Water Spirits

THE SAILOR BOY

He rose at dawn and, fired with hope,
  Shot o'er the seething harbour-bar,
And reach'd the ship and caught the rope,
  And whistled to the morning star.

And while he whistled long and loud
  He heard a fierce mermaiden cry;
'O boy, tho' thou art young and proud,
  I see the place where thou wilt lie.

'The sands and yeasty surges mix
  In caves about the dreary bay,
And on thy ribs the limpet sticks,
  And in thy heart the scrawl shall play.'

'Fool,' he answer'd, 'death is sure
  To those that stay and those that roam,
But I will nevermore endure
  To sit with empty hands at home.

'My mother clings about my neck,
  My sisters crying, "Stay for shame;"
My father raves of death and wreck,
  They are all to blame, they are all to blame.

'God help me! save I take my part
  Of danger on the roaring sea,
A devil rises in my heart,
  Far worse than any death to me.'

ALFRED, LORD TENNYSON

THE REVEREND
ARBUTHNOT-ARMITAGE-BROWN

The Reverend Arbuthnot-Armitage-Brown
  stood up to deliver a Sermon.
He was not aware that a Whale was there
  accompanied by a Merman.

'I consider this world a terrible place'
  he began. 'I consider the worm an
extremely unpleasant prospect to face.
  This is the text of my Sermon.'

But neither the Whale nor his friend could speak
  English or French or German
And so, though they heard, understood not a word
  Of the Reverend Et Cetera's sermon.

For eighty-five hours by the Church clock
  He spoke about ashes and vermin
and ghouls and souls and burial holes
  and graves with a bone and a worm in.

Till 'Come,' said the Whale to his friend, whose name
  Believe it or not, was Herman,
'This is no place for me. Let us go back to sea.
  Thank God I'm Whale and you're Merman.'

GEORGE BARKER

THE EDDYSTONE LIGHT

Me father was the keeper of the Eddystone Light,
He married a mer-my-aid one night;
Out of the match came children three –
Two was fish and the other was me.

Jolly stories, jolly told
When the winds is bleak and the nights is cold;
No such life can be led on the shore
As is had on the rocks by the ocean's roar.

When I was but a boyish chip,
They put me in charge of the old lightship;
I trimmed the lamps and I filled 'em with oil,
And I played Seven-up accordin' to Hoyle.

One evenin' as I was a-trimmin' the glim
An' singin' a verse of the evenin' hymn,
I see by the light of me binnacle lamp
Me kind old father lookin' jolly and damp;
An' a voice from the starboard shouted 'Ahoy!'
An' there was me gran'mother sittin' on a buoy –
Meanin' a buoy for ships what sail
An' not a boy what's a juvenile male.

Jolly stories, jolly told
When the winds is bleak and the nights is cold;
No such life can be led on the shore
As is had on the rocks by the ocean's roar.

ANONYMOUS

Seven-up: a card game

197

THE ISLES OF JESSAMY

'Twas on the good ship *Dollymop*
the crew made no attempt to stop
their Captain drinking hypnopop,
     known as The Sailor's Glee.

He climbed the mast and cried 'Hark! Hark! –
there goes the high-browed *Cutty Sark*,
quiet as the fin of a tiger shark
     across the sunlit sea.'

'Do not mislead us with your woe,
Dear Captain,' sighed the Mate, 'we know
the little shirt you mention-o,'
     (the crew wept openly),

'went down a thousand days ago,
with every stitch of calico,
and all aboard her lie below
     the Isles of Jessamy.'

Down from the mast the Captain flew
and doffed his bowler as he blew
over the far horizon's blue
     they heard his 'Goodbyeee . . .'

So now his crew sail down the lanes
above the great abyssal plains
where none can stay until he gains
     the Isles of Jessamy.

CHRISTOPHER LOGUE

COUNT ARNALDOS

Who ever will find such fortune
On the waters of the sea
As befell Count Arnaldos
On St John's Day morning?
As he was going hunting
With his hawk on his hand
He saw a galley
Making in for the land.
Its sails were of silk,
Of fine silk its rigging,
The sailor at the helm
Came singing a song
At which the sea grew smooth
And the winds became gentle,
And the fish that go in the deep
Came swimming to the top,
And the birds that go flying
Came to perch on the mast.
Then spoke Count Arnaldos,
You will hear what he said:
    'I beg you in God's name, sailor,
Repeat that song to me.'
The sailor made him answer,
This was his reply:
    'I repeat that song to no one
But to him who comes with me.'

TRADITIONAL SPANISH;
translated by W. S. Merwin

GLAUCUS

Ignorant of the hollow seas
in the green tides my body stands
lashed in the seaweed and the sands.
In the salt swell my yellow bones
beat on the sandy golden shore
noosed in the wet wrack and the weed.
The beat of inland bells my bones
moves in the shingle and the shell;
I hear the salt cry of the gull,
the wet slap of the sagging sail.
I hear the creaking of the tides
where in green seas my body stands.
I hear the inland beat of bells
about my bones and broken hands.
On the drowned altar where I bleed,
in the green pasture of the whale,
I hear the salt yell of the gull,
the sharp snap of the snapping sail.
I, the desolate rage of sea
tongue the tin-throated pilot bell:
I see the winds the waves divide,
I urge the loud disastrous swell,
and father the shipwrecking tide;
I am inhuman as the sea,
and as the fathering sea, divine:
wound in the shingle and the weed
to the drowned altar where I bleed
salt blood to the prodigious sea.

DAVID WRIGHT

Glaucus, in Greek mythology, was a fisherman who ate a magic herb and
became a sea-god able to foretell the future.

SABRINA FAIR

Sabrina fair,
   Listen where thou art sitting
Under the glassy, cool, translucent wave,
   In twisted braids of lilies knitting
The loose train of thy amber-dropping hair;
   Listen for dear honor's sake,
   Goddess of the silver lake,
   Listen and save.

JOHN MILTON
From *Comus*

Sabrina : a water-nymph, goddess of the River Severn

SABRINA'S SONG

By the rushy-fringèd bank,
Where grows the willow and the osier dank,
   My sliding chariot stays,
Thick set with agate, and the azurn sheen
   Of turkis blue, and emerald green,
     That in the channel strays,
   Whilst from off the waters fleet
   Thus I set my printless feet
   O'er the cowslip's velvet head,
     That bends not as I tread.
   Gentle swain, at thy request
     I am here.

JOHN MILTON
From *Comus*

turkis : turquoise

COLOGNE

In Köhln, a town of monks and bones,
And pavements fang'd with murderous stones,
And rags, and hags, and hideous wenches;
I counted two and seventy stenches,
All well defined, and several stinks!
Ye Nymphs that reign o'er sewers and sinks,
The river Rhine, it is well known,
Doth wash your city of Cologne;
But tell me, Nymphs, what power divine
Shall henceforth wash the river Rhine?

SAMUEL TAYLOR COLERIDGE

CREATURES
OF EARTH & AIR·····

THE CRACKLING TWIG

There came a satyr creeping through the wood,
His hair fell on his breast, his legs were slim:
His eyes were dancing wickedly, he stood,
He peeped about on every side of him.

He danced! He peeped! But, at a sound I made,
A crackling twig, he turned; and, suddenly,
In three great jumps, he bounded to the shade,
And disappeared among the greenery!

JAMES STEPHENS

satyr : a half-human, half-animal woodland god; a companion of Bacchus

NAN'S SONG

In Giant's Champflower where I was born
I would lie all night in the standing corn
Hearing the horses beyond the hay
Lift their heads in a friendly neigh.
    Those days are gone
    But the dream lives on.

Through fabulous bright moonlight nights
Those tossing manes, hooves silver bright
Rang on the cobbles of my sleep
And the gold of their foreheads burned deep, deep, deep.
    I woke and wept.
    I wake and weep.

So the unicorns with their manes a-lather
Seem gentle as my childhood father.
God forgive me, I'd be glad to rest
Those great gold heads upon my breast.
    'Be careful, maid!'
    I'm not afraid.

MAURICE CARPENTER
From *Unicorns*

THE TREE

Tree, lend me this root,
That I may sit here at your foot
And watch these hawking flies that wheel
And perch on the air's hand
And red-thighed bees
That fan the dust with their wings' breeze.
Do you not feel me on your heel,
My bone against your bone?
Or are you in such slumber sunk,
Woodpeckers knocking at your trunk
Find you are not at home?
To winds you are not dumb;
Then tell me, if you understand:
When your thick timber has been hewn,
Its boards in floors and fences sewn,
And you no more a tree,
Where will your dryad be?

ANDREW YOUNG

dryad: a nymph who lives in a tree

THE SOLDAN'S SONG

When green as a river was the barley,
Green as a river the rye,
I waded deep and began to parley
With a youth whom I heard sigh.
'I seek,' said he, 'a lovely lady,
A nymph as bright as a queen,
Like a tree that drips with pearls her shady
Locks of hair were seen;
And all the rivers became her flocks
Though their wool you cannot shear,
Because of the love of her flowing locks.
The kingly sun like a swain
Came strong, unheeding of her scorn,
Wading in deeps where she has lain,
Sleeping upon her river lawn
And chasing her starry satyr train.
She fled, and changed into a tree, –
That lovely fair-haired lady . . .
And now I seek through the sere summer
Where no trees are shady.'

EDITH SITWELL
From *The Sleeping Beauty*

OVERHEARD ON A SALTMARSH

Nymph, nymph, what are your beads?
Green glass, goblin. Why do you stare at them?
Give them me.
              No.
Give them me. Give them me.
                      No.
Then I will howl all night in the reeds,
Lie in the mud and howl for them.

Goblin, why do you love them so?

They are better than stars or water,
Better than voices of winds that sing,
Better than any man's fair daughter,
Your green glass beads on a silver ring.

Hush I stole them out of the moon.

Give me your beads, I desire them.
                    No.

I will howl in a deep lagoon
For your green glass beads, I love them so.
Give them me. Give them.
               No.

HAROLD MONRO

O HERE IT IS! AND THERE IT IS!

O here it is! And there it is!
And no one knows whose share it is
Nor dares to stake a claim –
But we have seen it in the air
A fairy like a William Pear –
With but itself to blame.

A thug it is – and smug it is
And like a floating pug it is
Above the orchard trees
It has no right – no right at all
To soar above the orchard wall
With chilblains on its knees.

MERVYN PEAKE

THE ANCIENT ELF

I am the maker,
The builder, the breaker,
The eagle-winged helper,
The speedy forsaker!

The lance and the lyre,
The water, the fire,
The tooth of oppression,
The lip of desire!

The snare and the wing,
The honey, the sting!
When you seek for me – look
For a different thing.

I, careless and gay,
Never mean what I say,
For my thoughts and my eyes
Look the opposite way!

JAMES STEPHENS

FAIRY STORY

I went into the wood one day
And there I walked and lost my way

When it was so dark I could not see
A little creature came to me

He said if I would sing a song
The time would not be very long

But first I must let him hold my hand tight
Or else the wood would give me a fright

I sang a song, he let me go
But now I am home again there is nobody I know.

STEVIE SMITH

THIS IS MAB, THE MISTRESS-FAIRY

This is Mab, the mistress-fairy,
That doth nightly rob the dairy,
And can hurt or help the churning
As she please, without discerning:

She that pinches country wenches
If they rub not clean their benches,
And with sharper nails remembers
When they rake not up their embers;
But if so they chance to feast her,
In a shoe she drops a tester.

This is she that empties cradles,
Takes out children, puts in ladles,
Trains forth midwives in their slumber
With a sieve the holes to number;
And then leads them from her boroughs
Home through ponds and water-furrows.

She can start our franklin's daughters
In their sleep with shrieks and laughters,
And on sweet Saint Anne's night
Feed them with a promised sight,
Some of husbands, some of lovers,
Which an empty dream discovers.

BEN JONSON
From *The Satyr*

tester: a coin; in Jonson's day, it was a sixpence
franklin: a landowner of free, not noble, birth

FAIRY'S SONG

Shed no tear – O shed no tear!
The flower will bloom another year.
Weep no more – O weep no more!
Young buds sleep in the root's white core.
Dry your eyes – O dry your eyes,
For I was taught in Paradise
To ease my breast of melodies –
        Shed no tear.

Overhead – look overhead
'Mong the blossoms white and red –
Look up, look up – I flutter now
On this flush pomegranate bough –
See me – 'tis this silvery bill
Ever cures the good man's ill –
Shed no tear – O shed no tear!
The flower will bloom another year.
Adieu – Adieu – I fly, adieu,
I vanish in the heaven's blue –
        Adieu, Adieu!

JOHN KEATS

WINE OF THE FAIRIES

I am drunk with the honey wine
Of the moon–unfolded eglantine,
Which fairies catch in hyacinth bowls.
The bats, the dormice, and the moles
Sleep in the walls or under the sward
Of the desolate castle yard;
And when 'tis split on the summer earth
　Or its fumes arise among the dew,
Their jocund dreams are full of mirth,
　They gibber their joy in sleep; for few
　Of the fairies bear those bowls so new!

PERCY BYSSHE SHELLEY

ARIEL'S SONG

Come unto these yellow sands,
　And then take hands:
Curtsied when you have, and kiss'd, –
　The wild waves whist, –
Foot it featly here and there;
And, sweet sprites, the burden bear,
　Hark, hark!
　Bow, wow,
　The watch-dogs bark:
　Bow, wow,
　Hark, hark! I hear
The strain of strutting Chanticleer
　Cry, cock-a-diddle-dow.

WILLIAM SHAKESPEARE
From *The Tempest*

FROM THE FORESTS AND HIGHLANDS

From the forests and highlands
  We come, we come;
From the river-girt islands,
  Where loud waves are dumb
  Listening to my sweet pipings.
The wind in the reeds and the rushes,
  The bees on the bells of thyme,
The birds on the myrtle bushes,
  The cicale above in the lime,
And the lizards below in the grass,
Were as silent as ever old Tmolus was,
Listening to my sweet pipings.

PERCY BYSSHE SHELLEY
From *Hymn of Pan*

SONG

O'er the smooth enameled green
Where no print of step hath been,
  Follow me as I sing,
  And touch the warbled string.
Under the shady roof
Of branching elm star-proof,
  Follow me;
I will bring you where she sits,
Clad in splendor as befits
  Her deity.
Such a rural Queen
All Arcadia hath not seen.

JOHN MILTON
From *Arcades*

THE FAIRY QUEEN

Come, follow, follow me,
  You, fairy elves that be:
  Which circle on the green,
  Come follow Mab your queen.
Hand in hand let's dance around,
For this place is fairy ground.

  When mortals are at rest,
  And snoring in their nest;
  Unheard, and un-espied,
  Through key-holes we do glide;
Over tables, stools and shelves.
We trip it with our fairy elves.

  And, if the house be foul
  With platter, dish or bowl,
  Up stairs we nimbly creep,
  And find the sluts asleep:
There we pinch their arms and thighs;
None escapes, nor none espies.

  But if the house be swept,
  And from uncleanness kept,
  We praise the household maid,
  And duly she is paid:
For we use before we go
To drop a tester in her shoe.

  Upon a mushroom's head
  Our table-cloth we spread;

A grain of rye, or wheat,
Is manchet, which we eat;
Pearly drops of dew we drink
In acorn cups fill'd to the brink.

The brains of nightingales,
With unctuous fat of snails,
Between two cockles stew'd,
Is meat that's easily chew'd;
Tails of worms, and marrow of mice
Do make a dish, that's wondrous nice.

The grasshopper, gnat, and fly,
Serve for our minstrelsy;
Grace said, we dance a while,
And so the time beguile;
And if the moon doth hide her head,
The gloe-worm lights us home to bed.

On tops of dewy grass
So nimbly do we pass,
The young and tender stalk
Ne'er bends when we do walk:
Yet in the morning may be seen
Where we the night before have been.

ANONYMOUS

manchet : finest white bread

WHOM THE UNTAUGHT SHEPHERDS CALL

Whom the untaught Shepherds call
   Pixies in their madrigal,
Fancy's children, here we dwell:
   Welcome, Ladies! to our cell.
Here the wren of softest note
   Builds its nest and warbles well;
Here the blackbird strains his throat:
   Welcome, Ladies! to our cell.

SAMUEL TAYLOR COLERIDGE
From *Songs of the Pixies*

EVENING BY EVENING

Evening by evening
Among the brookside rushes,
Laura bowed her head to hear,
Lizzie veiled her blushes:
Crouching close together
In the cooling weather,
With clasping arms and cautioning lips,
With tingling cheeks and finger tips.
'Lie close,' Laura said,
Pricking up her golden head:
'We must not look at goblin men,
We must not buy their fruits:
Who knows upon what soil they fed
Their hungry thirsty roots?'
'Come buy,' call the goblins
Hobbling down the glen.
'Oh,' cried Lizzie, 'Laura, Laura,
You should not peep at goblin men.'
Lizzie covered up her eyes,

Covered close lest they should look;
Laura reared her glossy head,
And whispered like the restless brook:
'Look, Lizzie, look, Lizzie,
Down the glen tramp little men.
One hauls a basket,
One bears a plate,
One lugs a golden dish
Of many pounds weight.
How fair the vine must grow
Whose grapes are so luscious;
How warm the wind must blow
Through those fruit bushes.'
'No,' said Lizzie: 'No, no, no;
Their offers should not charm us,
Their evil gifts would harm us'.
She thrust a dimpled finger
In each ear, shut eyes and ran:
Curious Laura chose to linger
Wondering at each merchant man.
One had a cat's face,
One whisked a tail,
One tramped at a rat's pace,
One crawled like a snail,
One like a wombat prowled obtuse and furry,
One like a ratel tumbled hurry-skurry.
She heard a voice like voice of doves
Cooing all together:
They sounded kind and full of loves
In the pleasant weather.

CHRISTINA ROSSETTI
From *Goblin Market*

ratel: an Indian and South African mammal rather like a weasel

NOW THE HUNGRY LION ROARS

Puck Now the hungry lion roars,
　　　And the wolf behowls the moon;
Whilst the heavy ploughman snores,
　　　All with weary task fordone.
Now the wasted brands do glow,
　　　Whilst the screech-owl, screeching loud,
Puts the wretch that lies in woe
　　　In remembrance of a shroud.
Now it is the time of night
　　　That the graves, all gaping wide,
Every one lets forth his sprite,
　　　In the church-way paths to glide:
And we fairies, that do run
　　　By the triple Hecate's team,
From the presence of the sun,
　　　Following darkness like a dream,
Now are frolic; not a mouse
Shall disturb this hallow'd house:
I am sent with broom before,
To sweep the dust behind the door.

WILLIAM SHAKESPEARE
From *A Midsummer Night's Dream*

Hecate : The Greek goddess of the dead, who taught witchcraft and magic.
She was sometimes shown as having three heads: that of a dog, of a horse,
and of a lion.

WHEN FADES THE MOON
TO SHADOWY-PALE

When fades the moon to shadowy-pale,
And scuds the cloud before the gale,
Ere the Morn all gem-bedight
Hath streak'd the East with rosy light,
We sip the furze-flower's fragrant dews
Clad in robes of rainbow hues;
Or sport amid the shooting gleams
To the tune of distant-tinkling teams,
While lusty Labour scouting sorrow
Bids the Dame a glad good-morrow,
Who jogs the accustom'd road along,
And paces cheery to her cheering song.

SAMUEL TAYLOR COLERIDGE
From *Songs of the Pixies*

ROBIN GOOD-FELLOW

From Oberon, in fairy land,
  The king of ghosts and shadows there,
Mad Robin I, at his command,
  Am sent to view the night-sports here.
    What revel rout
    Is kept about,
In every corner where I go,
    I will o'ersee,
    And merry be,
And make good sport, with ho, ho, ho!

More swift than lightning can I fly
  About this airy welkin soon,
And, in a minute's pace, descry
  Each thing that's done below the moon,
    There's not a hag
    Or ghost shall wag,
Or cry, ware Goblins! where I go:
    But Robin I
    Their feats will spy,
And send them home, with ho, ho, ho!

Whene'er such wanderers I meet,
  As from their night-sports they trudge home;
With counterfeiting voice I greet
  And call them on, with me to roam
    Thro' woods, thro' lakes,
    Thro' bogs, thro' brakes;

welkin: the sky

223

Or else, unseen, with them I go,
　　All in the nick
　　To play some trick
And frolic it, with ho, ho, ho!

Sometimes I meet them like a man;
　　Sometimes, an ox, sometimes, a hound;
And to a horse I turn me can;
　　To trip and trot about them round.
　　　　But, if, to ride,
　　　　My back they stride,
More swift than wind away I go,
　　O'er hedge and lands,
　　Thro' pools and ponds
I whirry, laughing, ho, ho, ho! . . .

When men do traps and engines set
　　In loop-holes, where the vermin creep,
Who from their folds and houses, get
　　Their ducks and geese, and lambs and sheep:
　　　　I spy the gin,
　　　　And enter in,
And seem a vermin taken so;
　　But when they there
　　Approach me near,
I leap out laughing, ho, ho, ho!

By wells and rills, in meadows green,
　　We nightly dance our hey-day guise;
And to our fairy king, and queen,
　　We chant our moonlight minstrelsies.

　　　　whirry: laugh
　　　　hey-day guise: country dances

When larks 'gin sing,
Away we fling;
And babes new born steal as we go,
And else in bed,
We leave instead,
And wend us laughing, ho, ho, ho!

From hag-bred Merlin's time have I
Thus nightly revell'd to and fro:
And for my pranks men call me by
The name of Robin Good-fellow.
Fiends, ghosts, and sprites,
Who haunt the nights,
The hags and goblins do me know;
And beldames old
My feats have told;
So *Vale*, *Vale*; ho, ho, ho!

ANONYMOUS
(extract)

Robin Good-Fellow, a mischievous sprite, is also Puck, son of Oberon, King of Fairyland. He is the fairies' clown or jester.
beldames : grandmothers

SONG OF THE GREMLINS

When you're seven miles up in the heavens
    And that's a heck of a lonely spot,
And it's 50 degrees below zero,
    Which isn't exactly hot,
When you're frozen blue like your Spitfire,
    And you're scared a Mosquito pink,
When you're thousands of miles from nowhere,
    And there's nothing below but the drink –
It's then you will see the gremlins,
    Green and gamboge and gold,
Male and female and neuter,
    Gremlins both young and old.

White ones'll wiggle your wing-tips,
    Male ones'll muddle your maps,
Green ones'll guzzle your glycol,
    Females will flutter your flaps,
Pink ones will perch on your perspex,
    And dance pirouettes on your prop.
There's one spherical middle-aged gremlin
    Who spins on your stick like a top.
They'll freeze up your camera shutters,
    They'll bite through your aileron wires,
They'll cause your whole tail to flutter,
    They'll insert toasting forks in your tyres.

This is the song of the gremlins
    As sung by the P.R.U.
Pretty ruddy unlikely to many,
    But fact none the less to the few.

ANONYMOUS, Royal Air Force Song, Second World War;
from a version by a Photographic Reconnaissance Unit

THE MERRY GUIDE

Once in the wind of morning
  I ranged the thymy wold;
The world-wide air was azure
  And all the brooks ran gold.

There through the dews beside me
  Behold a youth that trod,
With feathered cap on forehead,
  And poised a golden rod.

With mien to match the morning
  And gay delightful guise
And friendly brows and laughter
  He looked me in the eyes.

Oh whence, I asked, and whither?
  He smiled and would not say,
And looked at me and beckoned
  And laughed and led the way.

And with kind looks and laughter
  And nought to say beside
We two went on together,
  I and my happy guide.

Across the glittering pastures
  And empty upland still
And solitude of shepherds
  High in the folded hill,

By hanging woods and hamlets
That gaze through orchards down
On many a windmill turning
And far-discovered town,

With gay regards of promise
And sure unslackened stride
And smiles and nothing spoken
Led on my merry guide.

By blowing realms of woodland
With sunstruck vanes afield
And cloud-led shadows sailing
About the windy weald,

By valley-guarded granges
And silver waters wide,
Content at heart I followed
With my delightful guide.

And like the cloudy shadows
Across the country blown
We two fare on for ever,
But not we two alone.

With the great gale we journey
That breathes from gardens thinned,
Borne in the drift of blossoms
Whose petals throng the wind;

Buoyed on the heaven-heard whisper
Of dancing leaflets whirled
From all the woods that autumn
Bereaves in all the world.

And midst the fluttering legion
   Of all that ever died
I follow, and before us
   Goes the delightful guide,

With lips that brim with laughter
   But never once respond,
And feet that fly on feathers,
   And serpent-circled wand.

A. E. HOUSMAN

PAN WITH US

Pan came out of the woods one day, –
His skin and his hair and his eyes were grey,
The grey of the moss of walls were they, –
   And stood in the sun and looked his fill
   At wooded valley and wooded hill.

He stood in the zephyr, pipes in hand,
On a height of naked pasture land;
In all the country he did command
   He saw no smoke and he saw no roof.
   That was well! and he stamped a hoof.

His heart knew peace, for none came here
To this lean feeding save once a year
Someone to salt the half-wild steer,
   Or homespun children with clicking pails
   Who see so little they tell no tales.

He tossed his pipes, too hard to teach
A new-world song, far out of reach,
For a sylvan sign that the blue jay's screech
   And the whimper of hawks beside the sun
   Were music enough for him, for one.

Times were changed from what they were:
Such pipes kept less of power to stir
The fruited bough of the juniper
   And the fragile bluets clustered there
   Than the merest aimless breath of air.

They were pipes of pagan mirth,
And the world had found new terms of worth.
He laid him down on the sun-burned earth
   And ravelled a flower and looked away –
   Play? Play? – What should he play?

ROBERT FROST

230

INDEX OF FIRST LINES

INDEX OF AUTHORS

ACKNOWLEDGEMENTS

The editor and publishers wish to thank the following for permission to use copyright material in this collection:

Angus & Robertson (U.K.) Ltd for 'The Rogery Birds' and 'The Totem Pole' by Mary Gilmore, from *The Singing Tree*; George Allen & Unwin Ltd and Farrar, Straus & Giroux Inc. for 'A Small Dragon' by Brian Patten, from *Notes to the Hurrying Man*; © Brian Patten 1969 Margot Astrov for 'Rain Song', 'Curing Song', 'Song to Bring Fair Weather' and 'Plaint Against the Fog', from *American Indian Prose and Poetry* published by Putnam, New York; Patricia Beer for 'The Ghost'; Thomas Blackburn and The Hand & Flower Press for 'Drowned, Sir, drowned men the lot of them!'; Jonathan Cape Ltd, The Estate of Robert Frost and Holt, Rinehart & Winston Inc. for 'House Fear' and 'Pan With Us' from *The Poetry of Robert Frost* edited by Edward Connery Lathem. Copyright 1916, 1934 © 1969 by Holt, Rinehart & Winston Inc. Copyright 1944 © 1962 by Robert Frost; Jonathan Cape Ltd for 'Ardevora Veor' by A. L. Rowse, from *Strange Encounter*; Chatto & Windus Ltd for 'Stones' by Leslie Norris, from *Ransoms*, 'Carve her Name' by Michael Baldwin, from *Hob and other Poems*, 1972, 'The Roc' by Edward Lowbury, from *Green Magic*, 1972, 'Kingdom of Mist' by Edward Storey, from *North Bank Night*, 1969; Columbia University Press 1932 for 'Song of Two Ghosts', reprinted from *Fortune: Omaha Secret Societies*, New York by permission of the publisher; Leonard Clark and Secker & Warburg for 'The Tree' by Andrew Young, from *The Collected Poems of Andrew Young*; Jeni Couzyn and Workshop Press for 'The Soul is the Breath in your Body', from *Flying*; Andre Deutsch Ltd for 'A Boy's Friend' and 'The Start of A Memorable Holiday' by Roy Fuller from *Seen Grandpa Lately?*; The Devin-Adair Company, Connecticut and Oxford University Press for 'The Charm' by Padraic Colum from *Collected Poems of Padraic Colum*; Denis Dobson for 'Hallowe'en' by Leonard Clark, from *Good Company*; Gerald Duckworth & Co Ltd for 'Overheard on a Saltmarsh' by Harold Monro, from *The Silent Pool*; Enitharmon Press for 'Voices' and 'Ends Meet', from *Selected Poems* by Frances Bellerby 1971.

Faber & Faber Ltd and Harper & Row, Publishers Inc. for 'Robin Song' by Ted Hughes, from *Crow*; Faber & Faber Ltd and Random House Inc. for 'Song of the Ogres' by W. H. Auden, from *City Without Walls and other Poems*; Faber & Faber Ltd and Doubleday & Co Inc. for 'The Serpent', copyright 1950, by Theodore Roethke, from *The Collected Poems of Theodore Roethke*; Faber & Faber Ltd and John Johnson for 'This is a rune I have heard a tree say' by George Barker, from *Runes and Rhymes and Tunes and Chimes*; W. S. Graham for 'The Soldier Campion'; Faber & Faber Ltd for 'The Reverend Arbuthnot-Armitage-Brown' by George Barker, from *To Aylsham Fair*; William Heinemann Ltd for 'Spells' by James Reeves, from *The Wandering Moon*; and 'Magic Song for Him who wishes to Live' by Knud Rasmussen, from *Greenland by the Polar Sea*, translated by Asta and Rowland Kenney; David Higham Associates Ltd for

ACKNOWLEDGEMENTS

'The Chough' by John Heath-Stubbs, 'Tom Bone' and 'Colonel Fazackerley' from *Figgie Hobbin* by Charles Causley published by Macmillan; 'A Rare and Miraculous Case' and 'Count Arnaldos', translated by W. S. Merwin, from *Some Spanish Ballads* published by Hart-Davis, 'John Fane Dingle' by Richard Hughes, from *Glaucopis* published by Chatto & Windus; 'The Great Nemo' by Osbert Sitwell, from *Wrack at Tidesend* published by Macmillan; 'The Soldan's Song' and 'The Youth with the Red-Gold Hair', from *Collected Poems* by Edith Sitwell published by Macmillan.

The Hogarth Press Ltd for 'The Scarecrow in the Schoolmaster's Oats' by George Mackay Brown, from *Fishermen with Ploughs*; Hope Leresche & Steele for 'The Isles of Jessamy' © Christopher Logue 1972; Longman Group Ltd for 'Fairy Story' by Stevie Smith, from *Two In One*; Longman Group and New Directions Publishing Corporation for 'The Warden' by Stevie Smith, from *Selected Poems* © 1964 by Stevie Smith; Macmillan, London and Basingstoke, for 'Charm for Striking Fear into a Tiger and Hardening one's Own Heart' by Walter William Skeat, from *Malay Magic*, 'The Secret Brother' and 'Rhyme for Children' by Elizabeth Jennings, from *The Secret Brother*; Macmillan, London and Basingstoke, Macmillan Company of Canada Ltd, St Martin's Press Inc., New York and Mrs Hodgson for 'The Great Auk's Ghost' by Ralph Hodgson; the Trustees of the Hardy Estate, Macmillan London and Basingstoke, Macmillan Company of New York and Macmillan Company of Canada Ltd for 'On a Midsummer Eve' and 'The Glimpse' by Thomas Hardy, from *Collected Poems*; Mrs Iris Wise, Macmillan, London and Basingstoke, Macmillan Company of Canada, and Macmillan Company, New York, for 'In the Orchard', 'Check', 'The Ancient Elf' and 'The Crackling Twig' by James Stephens, from *Collected Poems* © 1915 the Macmillan Company, renewed 1943 by James Stephens.

John Murray and William Morrow & Co Inc. for 'Invocation of a Poet Seeking Inspiration', from *Return to the Islands* by Sir Arthur Grimble, © 1954, 1957 Olivia Grimble; John Murray (Publishers) Ltd and Houghton Mifflin Co. for 'City' and 'Lord Cozens Hardy' by John Betjeman, from *Collected Poems*; Novello & Co Ltd for 'I Saw a Strange Creature' translated by Kevin Crossley-Holland, from *Sun and Moon*; Peter Owen, London for 'O, here it is! And there it is!' and 'An old and crumbling parapet' by Mervyn Peake, from *A Book of Nonsense*; the Executors of the Estate of Harold Owen, Chatto & Windus and New Directions Publishing Corporation for 'Shadwell Stair', from *The Collected Poems of Wilfred Owen* edited by C. Day-Lewis (1963); Oxford University Press for 'Frutta di Mare', from *Poems* by Geoffrey Scott; 'Charm' and 'I would Sing Songs', from *Five Centuries of Polish Poetry 1450–1970* by Jerzy Peterkiewicz and Burns Singer with new poems translated in collaboration with Jon Stallworthy; Oxford University Press and James Reeves for 'The Three Singing Birds', from *The Blackbird in the Lilac*; Kathleen Raine for 'Spell of Creation', from *Collected Poems*; The Smithsonian Institution Press for 'Rattlesnake Ceremony Song', from *Hand-book of the Indians of California* by A. L. Kroeber; The Society of Authors as the literary representative of the Estate of John

ACKNOWLEDGEMENTS

Masefield and The Macmillan Company, New York, for 'Up on the Downs', from *Poems* © 1917, 1945; The Society of Authors as the literary representative of the Estate of A. E. Housman, Jonathan Cape Ltd and Holt, Rinehart & Winston Inc. for 'The Merry Guide', from 'A Shropshire Lad' – Authorised Edition – from *The Collected Poems of A. E. Housman*. Copyright 1939, 1940 © 1956 by Holt, Rinehart & Winston Inc. Copyright © 1967, 1968 by Robert E. Symons; and for 'Her Strong Enchantments Failing', from *The Collected Poems of A. E. Housman* copyright 1922 Holt, Rinehart & Winston Inc. Copyright 1950 by Barclays Bank Ltd.

The Literary Trustees of Walter de la Mare, and the Society of Authors as their representative, for 'The Three Beggars', 'The Witch', 'Hapless' and 'Dame Hickory', from *The Collected Poems of Walter de la Mare*, 1969, published by Faber & Faber; D. M. Thomas for 'Crickstone' and 'Twelve Men's Moor'; Maurice Carpenter for 'Nan's Song', from *Unicorns* edited by Montgomery and Harvey, published by Unicorn Literary Society, Bristol, 1960; Shirley Toulson for 'The Changeling'; University of Oklahoma Press for 'Aztec Song', from *The Aztecs: People of the Sun* by Alfonso Caso, translated by Lowell Dunham. Copyright 1958 University of Oklahoma Press.

Mr M. B. Yeats, Macmillan & Co Ltd and the Macmillan Company of Canada Ltd for 'The Stolen Child' and 'The Cap and Bells', from *The Collected Poems of W. B. Yeats*. Copyright 1906 by the Macmillan Company, renewed 1934 by William Butler Yeats.

Mrs George Bambridge for 'The Egg-Shell', 'Old Mother Laindinwool' and 'Cuckoo Song', from *The Definitive edition of Rudyard Kipling's Verse*; Robert Graves for 'Amergin's Charm' from *Collected Poems*, 1965, and 'Dicky', from *The Penny Fiddle*, and David Wright for 'Glaucus', from *Poems*.

For suggestions and assistance in the compilation of this anthology, the editor wishes to thank particularly Mr Ted Hughes, Miss Naomi Lewis, Professor the Rev. Canon W. Moelwyn Merchant, Mr John Moat, Miss Eileen O'Connor, Mrs Brenda Pike, Miss Janice Brent and Mrs Doreen Scott (of Penguin Books Ltd), Mr D. M. Thomas, Mr Alan Tucker, and the Librarians and staffs o. the Cornwall County Library (Launceston Branch), of the City of Plymouth Central Library, and of the University of Exeter.